Computerized
Maintenance Management
Systems

Computerized Maintenance Management Systems

SECOND EDITION

Terry Wireman

Industrial Press Inc.

Library of Congress Cataloging-in-Publication Data

Wireman, Terry.
    Computerized maintenance management systems / Terry Wireman.—
2nd ed.
    192p. 15.6 x 23.5 cm.
    Includes index.
    ISBN 0-8311-3054-7
    1. Plant maintenance—Data processing. 2. Industrial equipment—
Maintenance and repair—Data processing. I. Title.
TS192.W55   1994
658.2′02′0285—dc20   94-2509
                                          CIP

Industrial Press
200 Madison Avenue
New York, New York 10016–4078

**COMPUTERIZED MAINTENANCE
MANAGEMENT SYSTEMS
Second Edition**

FIRST PRINTING

2   4   6   5   3

Contents

Preface

Industry today is in a fight to survive. Competition is found not only on a domestic level, but also on international levels. In an effort to survive, all forms of production analysis, product reviews, and material reviews are made and periodically checked. Statistical process control is only one of the new methods used to reduce operational costs. However, one area many industries are now turning their attention toward is the maintenance function. While this function is often viewed as a necessary evil, it is also the last major area of cost reduction in both the public and private sectors.

Cost reduction in maintenance does not necessarily mean a reduction in service or in the quality of service. It means a better control of the maintenance organization and the related areas. To properly control the maintenance of any facility, information is required to analyze what is occurring. Manually, this requires a tremendous amount of effort and time. In recognition of this, many of the progressive companies are developing and using computer programs geared toward control of the maintenance organization. These systems are often referred to as computerized maintenance management systems (CMMS).

This book is designed to assist anyone who is investigating the possibility of using a computer in the maintenance function. It provides the information necessary to successfully evaluate, select, and implement a CMMS. If the information in this text is carefully applied during the installation, it will provide a successful and cost-effective solution to most maintenance problems.

Maintenance Management Objectives

Maintenance Management Objectives

This chapter will discuss the goals and objectives of all maintenance organizations. Certain groups may have some additional objectives; however, this listing will provide coverage of the standard objectives.

Primary Functions

To properly examine the computerized maintenance management systems, one should have an understanding of the maintenance function and its purpose in industry. The operational organization's prime responsibility is to produce a quality product on time and economically. The maintenance department has a more involved list of functions or responsibilities. These can be grouped in five main areas, as listed below.

Maintenance of Existing Equipment

Maintaining existing equipment is the basic reason for the department. The maintenance group will make repairs to the production equipment as quickly and economically as possible. They should be able to anticipate repairs, based on previous experience with the equipment. To prevent rapid wear of the equipment, the group should utilize cost-effective preventive maintenance programs.

To perform these tasks as efficiently and cost effectively as possible requires the utilization of a trained workforce and the use of modern tools and maintenance methods that are available. However, performing all of the above tasks depends on one important item—accurate record keeping. Without accurate records, it will not be possible to complete the assigned tasks in a timely and cost-effective manner.

Equipment Inspections and Service

This task will require the engineer or manufacturer to determine the proper lubricant for the equipment. In addition to the type of lubricant, the proper amount and time intervals of application of the lubricant are necessary. The inspections are required to ensure that the equipment is in safe operating condition and is being serviced in a timely manner.

Some installations will require that the operational personnel do some routine lubrication and servicing. Even where this is a common practice, the maintenance department should oversee the completion of the tasks.

Equipment Installation

This responsibility varies from industry to industry and depends on the size of the installation and the maintenance workforce. Some industrial facilities that require constant equipment changeover may have an installation department. When large installation projects occur in some industries without the necessary workforce, outside contractors are used to supply the needed manpower.

Maintenance Storekeeping

This responsibility of the maintenance group involves the receiving and distribution of the spares necessary for the repair and upkeep of the plant equipment. There are several important tasks involved in this responsibility. The first is recording the necessary spares for each piece of equipment. With all of the spares recorded, the maintenance group has the responsibility of setting the inventory level for each part. As the spares are used, the replacements will have to be ordered.

The ordering process is important to prevent material outages in the stores. Material outages could result in production delays, if equipment breakdowns occur and no replacement parts are available. Keeping the stores inventory level as low as possible will prevent tying up capital investments in spares.

Craft Administration

This is the responsibility of controlling the manpower used by the maintenance department. The most cost-effective way of determining the size of the workforce is the work in the maintenance backlog. By looking in the backlog, the number of employees for each craft area can easily be determined. As programs are changed and equipment is added or deleted from a department, the workforce can be adjusted as necessary. The responsibility for providing the necessary tools and supplies for the crafts is also included in this area.

Organizational Principles

In examining the organizational principles for maintenance, it is necessary to look at the following objectives set before the maintenance group.

1. Keep the maintenance cost for product or service as low as possible.
2. Meet the quality requirements of the product.
3. Meet the availability requirements for critical equipment.

4. Keep the maintenance costs as low as possible for noncritical equipment.
5. Provide and maintain adequate facilities for the operation.
6. Provide effective and trained supervision.

Once the major objectives are set before the maintenance management, it will be up to this group to set the policies for the department. These policies will all contribute to the accomplishment of the previously mentioned objectives.

One of the first policies should be the allocation of employee resources. The allocation of the resources will begin with the goals for scheduling.

Maintenance Scheduling

No maintenance schedule can be 100% effective. Unforeseen equipment breakdowns and work requests will reduce the efficiency of the schedule. Still, a good maintenance schedule should achieve 70–90% efficiency. (Some higher efficiency figures are achieved using the computerized scheduling systems.)

Most effective scheduling programs schedule maintenance work with a lead time of 1 week. Any less time is inefficient. Schedules made out with more than 1 week lead time will be changed due to emergency and breakdown work requests, which ultimately change the priority of the scheduled jobs.

Work Requests

The maintenance policy should also include the proper steps to initiate work requests. These requests should have a specific routing for approval. Once approved, the work requests should have a priority rating assigned. These ratings should use standard guidelines agreed to by both the operating and maintenance departments. This priority rating will be used to determine how quickly a maintenance request will receive attention.

Another policy decision that will be made for each piece of equipment is whether it will be serviced by preventive maintenance or by breakdown (emergency) maintenance. The relationship curve between preventive maintenance and breakdown maintenance shows that the more breakdown maintenance is performed, the more costly the maintenance activity. The more preventive action is undertaken, the lower the maintenance cost.

The cost of preventive maintenance must be weighed against the cost of a resulting breakdown. For some equipment, it is more economical to service it only when it breaks down, rather than investing the manpower and materials to perform preventive maintenance. If the costs of preventive maintenance are greater than or equal to the cost that would be incurred by a breakdown, then preventive maintenance would be a waste of money.

Workforce

Another policy decision will be made about the type of workforce to employ. The choice is between using internal employees or outside contract employees to perform the work. Five points to consider when making this decision are:

1. type of work
2. skills of employees available
3. how fast the work needs to be accomplished
4. security of the installation
5. whether the plant is union or nonunion.

The type of workforce used is also determined by the production process. If the process is a 24-hour-per-day operation, maintenance personnel will have to be provided around the clock.

Some management policies limit the number of workers on the second and third shifts, and place most of the emphasis on maintenance during the day shift. The heaviest concentration of manpower is on the day shift, thus allowing for better work controls. This follows the successful pattern used by the Japanese industries.

Controls

Policies also have to detail certain controls for the smooth and efficient operation of the organization. One of the controls must be on the flow of paperwork. Sufficient paperwork is important to track certain areas of maintenance; however, excessive paperwork can slow the maintenance process by requiring too much detail and communication.

It is beneficial to design a series of standard communication forms for reporting processes. These standard forms will let all employees and supervisors know what information is required by management.

As management begins to establish cost controls, they should give supervisors and the superintendents the responsibility for controlling cost areas for which they are held accountable. An example would be the maintenance supervisor. If the supervisor is held accountable for the man-hours spent per unit of work (as an efficiency rating), then the supervisor should be given control over the craftsmen performing the work. If a superintendent is rated on the cost of the maintenance compared to the cost of the equipment maintained, then the superintendent should be given control over the factors that make up the maintenance costs.

Those are two examples of rating or evaluating maintenance supervisors. Other cost comparisons that require record keeping are the cost of maintenance labor compared to the maintenance materials and the percentage of equipment downtime to the equipment uptime (or runtime).

Maintenance Work and Cost Reporting

The ultimate goal of any industrial facility is to earn a profit. Earning a profit means close monitoring of all financial transactions and charges. To properly set the policies of the maintenance group, reports are needed. In the maintenance group, there are several areas of cost monitoring. Two of the most important are cost of labor and cost of materials. The labor charges will help to chart the manpower requirements; this is important where overtime is used. Overtime can be very costly. If controls are not exercised, then the costs can become excessive.

The material costs are usually for replacement parts for the equipment. Proper servicing of the equipment may help to reduce this cost. Monitoring this cost can be used to help justify maintenance expenditures.

Types of Work

To properly balance the maintenance workload, an analysis can be made of the types of work being performed. This analysis can be made by looking at the actual hours spent on each type of work (or in percentages of work). Common areas of importance are:

1. repair work
2. service work
3. preventive maintenance
4. emergency or breakdown work
5. work performed by operators.

Monitoring these costs will help in scheduling workloads and determining efficiencies.

Equipment Reports

Equipment reports should provide the following two types of data:

1. maintenance repair costs
2. history repair records.

The maintenance repair costs will include the maintenance materials used and the maintenance man-hours required for the repairs. These records will help identify equipment that is costly to maintain, or that requires excessive maintenance. Comparing the costs of similar equipment may help in solving repair and cost problems.

The history repair records will keep information about the types of repairs and what was actually done to the equipment. Looking at this information will help to pinpoint equipment requiring excessive emergency maintenance or receiving insufficient preventive maintenance. It also helps to spot repetitive problems with the equipment, so that they can be investigated and solved, further reducing costs. The information from the history should be available in an average time between failures (MTBF) and an average time to effect each repair (MTTR).

Backlog Reports

By keeping an active file of all work orders, it is easy to look through the file, sort by priority, and pinpoint problem areas as they develop. Use of the backlog can help to establish staffing levels and reduce unnecessary overhead.

Preventive Maintenance

The policy needs clear definition in the area of preventive maintenance. The policy must be set as to which equipment is going to have a preventive maintenance service and which equipment is not. Equipment failures and breakdowns occur in a pattern called the "bath tub curve." This curve helps us understand the preventive maintenance frequency for some equipment.

There are some serious points to consider when setting up a preventive maintenance program. These include the following.

1. What to inspect? All equipment or just that above a certain cost level; or only equipment critical to the plant operation and safety?
2. What to inspect for? How detailed are the inspections to be? How sophisticated will the testing equipment be? How much training will the inspector require?
3. When to inspect the equipment? Some equipment may be inspected according to the calendar, and others by a timer or operational meter reading. Which will the inspection use?
4. How much paperwork will be required? Many keep very detailed records, while others keep only necessary information. Which will the program require?

All of the above points should be carefully considered and incorporated into preventive maintenance record keeping. Details of when the equipment was last serviced is very important in helping to determine proper scheduling, and whether additional preventive maintenance could have prevented some breakdown.

Additional Controls

Additional controls are required in the matter of work request initiations. There are three important items, as follows:

1. authorization
2. priority
3. time and cost estimates.

Authorization is important to prevent unwanted or unnecessary work orders from being issued and worked on. The authorization will keep the work orders limited to the necessary work only, and this work will be accomplished in an efficient manner. An authorization is especially useful in expensive and complex work requests.

Priorities will help to ensure that important work is performed before less important work. There are at least five priority codes that could be used:

1. emergency
2. critical (within 24 hours)
3. repetitive
4. major repair or shutdown
5. preventive maintenance.

Some consultants recommend a multiplier-style priority scale. They divide the priorities into two categories—priority class and machine code. These classes are rated from 1 to 10. By multiplying the two ratings together, a single priority rating is achieved.

The priority class is the relative importance of the work requested. This runs from a high of 10 (breakdown or safety) to a low of 1 (which may be something like housekeeping). The machine code is the relative importance of the equipment to the production operation. This runs from a high of 10 (electrical distribution to plant) to a low of 1 (which is a machine or office not directly influencing production). By taking a work request for a safety job (10) on a piece of electrical distribution system for the plant supply (10), and multiplying them together, a relative importance status number of 100 is achieved. This indicates that the work order would receive the highest priority. If the work request was for a housekeeping assignment (1) in a nonproduction location (1), the relative importance status number would be 1. This would be a work order of the lowest priority. All other work orders would fall in between these two extremes. It is the responsibility of the plant management to code the equipment as to its relative importance to the production process. It will be up to the maintenance and production departments to decide on the priority class of the work request.

It is also possible to use a floating priority system which depends on the particular equipment involved in a production process during a given time period. Once this time period ends, another piece of production equipment could receive a higher rating.

Time estimates are important for the work requests to give practical estimates of the time required to perform the work, and how long the equipment will be out of service to perform the maintenance. These estimates should be as realistic as possible to assist in scheduling. Cost estimates are necessary to help budget work order costs. Estimates will also help determine who can authorize the work request.

Maintenance Stores Controls

To properly control the stores and inventory, the following points must be considered.

1. Are the parts listed by stock numbers?
2. Is the quantity-on-hand information readily available?
3. When an item is ordered, is the promised date noted so that the work can be tentatively scheduled?
4. Are the item prices available for stock items?

5. Can items be entered and removed from the stores as needed?

These questions will help stimulate thinking about reducing or controlling costs for the stores. If the stores inventory is too high, much needed capital may be tied up unnecessarily. Effective stores records containing information about equipment spares, cross reference spares, and spares item prices are important in determining the effectiveness of stores. All costs that can be reduced without causing equipment delays waiting on spares should be made.

Budgets

There are two general goals for any maintenance cost systems, as follows:

1. to provide accounting with their required information for accurate bookkeeping
2. to provide production departments with the information necessary for internal control and performance evaluation.

In the majority of organizations, there are five categories of maintenance expense:

1. capital improvements
2. general maintenance
3. equipment removal
4. utility production and distribution
5. miscellaneous expenses.

Capital Improvements

This category may be broad, and certain items will change from industry to industry. A completely new piece of equipment is considered a capital expense whether it is purchased or built in-house. The size of and amount spent on the equipment is the determining factor as to whether it is considered a capital expense in some industries. Generally, if it is given a life for depreciation and amortization, it is considered a capital expense.

Other types of expenses that may fit into this category include alterations, modernizations, or changes (usually structural) to a piece of equipment that increase its durability, productivity, or efficiency. This type of expense will prolong the useful life of an existing facility.

One additional type is a replacement. A replacement would not merely involve substituting a part or series of parts on a piece of equipment, which might occur as a result of preventive maintenance; the replacement of a kind of unit or major part should result in a longer useful life of the equipment. In some industries, this may also be called shutdown, retrofit, or outage maintenance.

General Maintenance

This category of expense includes all expenditures used to keep the plant and its equipment in satisfactory operating condition. Included in this category is emergency, critical, and preventive maintenance.

Emergency and critical maintenance is performed on the equipment just before or just after it has broken down. Generally, emergency maintenance is classified as maintenance performed when life, equipment, or the product is in jeopardy. If this maintenance is not performed immediately, irreparable damage may result. Critical maintenance is generally maintenance that must be performed within the next 24 hours to prevent it from becoming an emergency situation.

Preventive maintenance (and, in some industries, predictive maintenance) is the other category of general maintenance. Preventive maintenance may include inspections, minor adjustments and repairs, and lubrication. Preventive maintenance may even include cleaning and painting. This expense should be tracked to ensure that PM is not costing more than the equipment's actual value.

The maintenance expenses in these categories should be

tracked and kept separate from the other parts of the maintenance budgets, since these are the true source of maintenance expense. If they are not separated, it will not allow for an accurate comparison of actual maintenance costs, and will inflate and distort the actual costs with the expense of nonmaintenance activities.

Equipment Removal

This classification is the cost of removing any obsolete or unused equipment. It is generally only used when the entire unit of equipment is removed. In recent times, most sites have used outside contractors to perform this removal. Occasionally, when the equipment is sold, the buyer will furnish the manpower to remove the equipment to reduce actual costs.

Utility Production and Distribution

Plant-wide utilities generally include steam, electric power, water, compressed air, and natural gas. At some sites, sewers are considered an additional utility. The costs for the utilities are spread throughout the plant as a service to the production departments. When this occurs, the utility costs should not be a part of the maintenance expense. However, the repair costs involved in maintaining the utilities are considered a true maintenance expense.

Estimating Budgets

Maintenance budgets can be estimated by considering historical information on equipment costs. If the equipment costs for last year were at a certain level, allowing for inflation, they should be at about the same level for the next year. The record-keeping system should also allow the planned budget to be compared to the actual budget on a monthly basis. This will help spot cost overruns and allow logical steps to be taken to prevent any future overruns.

Each of the categories of maintenance costs can be divided into the following sections:

1. equipment
2. supplies
3. labor
4. outside services
5. maintenance overhead
6. plant overhead.

Equipment is considered to be those items that are purchased as a unit, or even produced in the plant shops as a complete assembly.

Supplies are those items carried in the maintenance or plant stores. They may be incorporated as components in the larger shop-fabricated equipment, in which case they lose their status as a supply and become part of the equipment. The reports should differentiate between the equipment and the supplies.

Labor is normally considered only to be the time spent by the craftsmen in the actual performance of the work requested.

The outside services are generally in the form of labor (contract) or expertise purchased through a contractor or even a supplier. Also included in this group are equipment rentals or engineering services.

Maintenance overhead includes all expenses that cannot be directly charged to specific work requests. At some sites, supervision and engineering services are accumulated and charged as maintenance overhead, while at other sites, they are charged against specific jobs. Other costs that may be included in maintenance overhead are depreciation of machine tools; cost of supplies such as drills, files, and gloves; insurance; and vacation credits. Some sites will also include maintenance's share of building rent, heating, and other utilities.

Plant overhead includes administrative costs that must be absorbed by all departments, including maintenance. Management salaries, service organizations, as well as any expense that is required for plant operation which cannot be allocated to a specific department, make up the plant overhead part of the maintenance cost.

Cost Reporting

Once the information has been recorded, in order to be useful, it must be compiled into a system that can provide up-to-date information to maintenance at any time. However, the information must also be in a form that is acceptable to the accounting department. In general, the information should meet the following requirements.

1. It should provide a measure of the effectiveness of the utilization of manpower and material.
2. It should provide an indication of the cost trends so areas needing attention can be spotted early.
3. It should provide information so that equipment having unusual maintenance costs can be identified.
4. It should allow production to identify all maintenance costs by product or equipment.

This information depends on the methods used to obtain and sort it. If care is taken in forming the reporting function, the needs of all involved will be met.

Common Reports

Two reports that are useful in monitoring the maintenance costs are the actual-versus-budget report and the variance report. The actual-versus-budget report will plot the budget for each department or cost center for the month. It will then plot the actual maintenance costs in labor, material, and "other" against the budget. This allows the manager to see how close to budget the plant is operating. Since it provides a breakdown of the costs, it should help spot the area of maintenance expense that is causing problems.

The variance report is used to list all of the departments or cost centers that are over budget. This report will allow the manager to concentrate his or her efforts in only the problem areas and not areas within their budgets. If the same breakdown of costs is given as in the above report, it makes it simpler to find the reasons for overruns.

The Maintenance Audit

This section describes a comprehensive audit of the maintenance function, followed by a procedure to correct any of the deficiencies uncovered by the audit.

Performance Audit

The audit should begin with a performance evaluation of all personnel involved in the maintenance function. The following areas should be considered:

1. job knowledge
2. performance
3. attitude
4. initiative
5. ingenuity
6. versatility
7. tact
8. leadership
9. ability to get along with others
10. resourcefulness
11. absenteeism
12. general health.

For those in supervisory positions, the following should be included:

13. organizational ability
14. managerial performance
15. administrative capability.

The rating should be on a scale of 1–10. When the findings are analyzed, they should be discussed with the employee. Counseling may be necessary on specific performance points. If a general weakness is noted throughout the organization, a general training program may be in order.

Maintenance Controls

The following four questions are important to consider in this area.

1. Is the maintenance utilization report used?
2. Is maintenance absenteeism closely tracked?
3. Does overtime exceed 5% of the total man-hours worked?
4. Are outside contractors used for routine jobs?

The answer should be "yes" to the first two questions, and "no" to the last two. If not, then action needs to be taken in the indicated area. The planning and control areas should be firmed up, with the emphasis placed on improved planning and increased craft effectiveness. If employees are not being effectively used, the planning and scheduling functions must be closely scrutinized. Improvements must be made if productivity is to increase.

If overtime is excessive, it indicates a "fire-fighting" situation. This reactive style of maintenance is not cost effective. More emphasis on PM and planned maintenance will help the situation.

The use of outside contractors on routine or standing jobs is a waste of resources. If the workload is such that the routine jobs cannot be covered by the permanent staff, then the staff should be increased. This will allow the contract workers to be used on outages or other large projects.

Maintenance Supervisor Activities

The supervisor's basic responsibilities should include analyzing the following.

1. Matching maintenance skills to the work requests.
2. Analyzing the maintenance skills available for the work request.
3. Controlling the job interruptions due to emergency requests.

4. Preventing work delays for reasons such as no spares, etc.
5. Ensuring that the work performed is of acceptable quality.
6. Ensuring that the work requests are completed in a timely manner.

The maintenance supervisor should have sufficient staff support so that 60% or more of his or her time is available for job followup.

The following activities should not be performed by the maintenance supervisor.

1. Preparing work schedules.
2. Controlling inventories of stores materials, tools, or equipment.
3. Receiving, recording, and prioritizing work orders.
4. Gathering and providing manuals, blueprints, sketches, or engineering diagrams to the craftsmen.
5. Recording or processing equipment repair records or check sheets.

If these activities are regularly performed by the maintenance supervisor, then additional staff support should be considered to allow the supervisor to devote the necessary amount of time to the duties that should be performed.

Analysis of Maintenance Charges

There are several questions that must be answered in this area.

1. Is all maintenance labor being charged to the correct department?
2. Does the work order system track the work, craft requirements, and backlog for each department?

The work order system presently in use should be used to charge the correct department with labor material and other charges related to the work orders.

There should not be a shortcut-type approach to the charge system. If incorrect information is kept, budget analysis, labor requirement projections, work backlogs, etc., will be meaningless. For proper tracking of maintenance costs, proper records must be kept.

Maintenance Stores Inventory

The maintenance stores contribute to delays and unnecessary downtime by inefficient stores procedures in stocking the parts and materials necessary to maintain the facilities equipment. Many locations have parts sitting on shelves gathering dust while equipment is down waiting on other spares.

The following questions should be asked when considering the maintenance stores.

1. Is the maintenance inventory secure?
2. Is it easy to obtain the total value of the inventory?
3. Can the availability of material be determined before the work is actually scheduled?
4. Is a system presently available that can pinpoint the location of the materials to ensure that they exist?
5. Can unused parts and materials be re-entered into the stores inventory when the work is completed?
6. Is the availability of all tools, equipment, and component assemblies readily determined?

If the answers to any of the above questions are "no," then attention should be given to those areas to help increase the efficiency of the stores. While manual systems may provide adequate control for smaller inventories, larger inventories should be computerized to gain the maximum cost savings from this area.

Maintenance Backlog

This is a key area for determining the effectiveness of a maintenance department. Some areas that develop problems in this area include poor work order planning, poor record keeping, and poor scheduling practices. The following questions should be asked while considering the maintenance backlog.

1. Does the backlog forecast the required downtime?
2. Is the work prioritized for each craft?
3. Are the priorities properly applied and reliable?
4. Is the backlog used to control the size of the workforce?

The answers to the questions should reflect the condition of the work order backlog. The work requests should be planned and scheduled each day. The schedules should reflect the consideration of the priorities, the required completion dates, the availability of craftworkers, materials, and equipment.

If the backlog is a problem, assigning accountability for the different functions should help to eliminate the problem.

It must be remembered that old habits die hard. If the maintenance function has not operated at a high efficiency for many years, the aforementioned changes will not be easy to implement. A gradual implementation program is recommended. This will help to ease out old habits.

The Maintenance Audit—
Part 2 (Detailed)

1. Utilization and Performance

A. What is the present utilization?
B. What is the present performance?
C. What is the present method level?
D. What is the present productivity?

(*Note:* After establishing the percentages for each of the above areas, multiply A, B, C, and D together to achieve the total maintenance productivity.)

E. Are the buildings and grounds well kept?
F. Are machines such as pumps, trucks, cranes, and other production equipment well kept?
G. Are the buildings and equipment inspected annually to determine if a change in PM inspections is necessary?
H. Does the annual budget include:

    1. Inspections?
    2. Scheduled overhauls or turnarounds?
    3. Historical projections?
    4. PM budgets?

2. Staffing and Policy

    A. Is an organization chart presently in use?

        1. Is it up to date?
        2. Do all positions have job descriptions?

    B. Are there job descriptions for each craft?
    C. What is the ratio of hourly to salary personnel?
    D. Do the following support positions exist:

        1. Planner?
        2. Scheduler?
        3. Material coordinator?
        4. Stores?
        5. Maintenance or plant engineer(s)?
        6. Training coordinator?

    E. Is the staff adequate, capable, and experienced?
    F. Are the maintenance supervisors responsible for 8–14 craftsmen?
    G. Are the supervisors spending 6 hours per shift with their employees?
    H. Is a work order or a work request system being used?

        1. Planning work orders over a given amount?
        2. Minor work charged to standing work orders?

    I. Is the work order process understood by all involved?
    J. Are all work orders screened by a competent, authorized individual?
    K. Does the work order system have a priority rating system?
    L. Does emergency work account for less than 5% of the total work?
    M.Is net capacity scheduling used?
    N. Is the backlog kept in man-hours per craft?

    O. Is the backlog purged quarterly to eliminate work no longer required?

    P. Is there a weekly schedule meeting involving production and maintenance to plan the following week's work?

    Q. Is the backlog used to determine staffing levels?

3. Supervisory and Craft Training

    A. Are there training programs for:

        1. Maintenance management?
        2. Maintenance supervisors?
        3. Hourly employees?
        4. Maintenance support personnel?

    B. Is there any productivity training?

        1. Work simplification?
        2. Method improvement techniques?
        3. Basic work analysis?
        4. Labor relations instructions?
        5. Communications and delegation?

    C. How is the training conducted?
    D. Is there a formal craft training program?
    E. How is the craft training conducted?
    F. Are there minimum job skill requirements for each position?
    G. Are the department needs satisfied by the apprentice training program?
    H. Do the supervisors and craftworkers receive regular technical training?
    I. Do all employees attend one safety meeting per month?
    J. Is the maintenance safety record improving?
    K. Are monthly safety inspections made?
    L. Are all maintenance materials removed from a job site within 24 hours?
    M. Do all employees use the prescribed safety equipment?

4. Planner Training

    A. Is a planner function used?

    B. Is there formal planner training?

5. Motivation

    A. How is the labor/management relationship?

    B. Is there a skill/rate problem on substandard performance?

    C. What is the annual craft and supervisor turnover?

6. Negotiations

    A. Was there a strike prior to the last contract settlement?

    B. What is your level and procedure for grievances?

    C. What is the percentage of grievances settled?

7. Controls, Budgets, and Costs

    A. Are any of the following used for maintenance control?

        1. Shop floor work measurement?

        2. Budgets?

        3. Historical costs?

    B. Which of the following are considered when monitoring trends?

        1. Percent of downtime?

        2. Percent of performance?

        3. Planner coverage?

        4. Cost per hour for maintenance?

        5. Percentage of productivity?

        6. Hours of backlog?

        7. Overtime hours?

    C. How much time elapses between the end of job time and report generation?

    D. How often are reports generated?

    E. How is job time and work reported?

F. How is the information on the report summarized?

G. Who receives the reports?

H. What percentage of man-hours is covered by written work orders?

I. What percentage of these hours is blanket work orders?

J. What percentage of work orders has enough time to be properly planned?

K. Is all shutdown work preplanned?

L. Are all labor and materials estimated before work begins (except for emergencies)?

M. Are there repetitive work order standards?

N. Is there an authorization system?

O. Do all individuals who authorize work receive a report showing the labor and material charges?

P. Are all major variances from estimates investigated, and are explanations made for the variance?

Q. Is the maintenance work performed charged to the operating department requesting the work?

R. Are all high-maintenance equipment items tracked, and are reasons for high maintenance costs explained?

S. Is there a maintenance staff meeting held on a regular basis to discuss methods of reducing costs?

8. Facilities

A. Is there a current plant floor plan?

B. Are the maintenance shop layouts practical and efficient?

C. How is the shop housekeeping?

D. Are proper safety equipment and signs always used?

E. What is the condition of the equipment and tools?

F. Is there adequate office space for supervisors and staff?

G. How is the lighting?

H. Are utility systems (gas, water, air, electric) inspected and serviced annually?

9. Stores and Materials

A. Is there an up-to-date stores catalog?

B. Is there a perpetual inventory system for major items and spares?

C. Is a withdrawal or issue slip required for each transaction?

D. Is there a list of tools that the company and the craftsman must provide?

E. How many tools are out of service for repair?

F. Are the EOQ's calculated for the items in stores?

G. What percentage of the materials ordered is received on time?

H. Does purchasing track the delivery times and dates of important equipment items?

I. Are lead times provided to maintenance for all necessary spares?

J. Does purchasing carefully select vendors by rating their quality of service?

K. Does maintenance provide the max–min levels for all maintenance items?

L. Are all stores items accounted for in the inventory process?

M. Is there an annual review of obsolete stock items for possible deletion?

N. Can stores materials be reserved for planned work orders?

O. Is there a list of what equipment each item is used on?

P. Does the stores inventory show a current amount on hand for all stock items?

Q. Do A and B items make up 95% of stores stock costs?

　　1. A = 15–25% of stores items comprising 70–80% of the stores annual value.

　　2. B = 15–25% of stores items comprising 20% of the stores annual value.

10. PM and Equipment History

A. What percentage of major equipment has a recorded repair history?

B. Are the equipment history records reviewed at least once a year?

C. What percent of the equipment is covered by a PM routine?

D. What equipment is covered by the following:

1. Downtime trend report
2. PM compliance with schedules
3. Compliance with written PM instructions.

E. Is the equipment history kept for at least 2 years, including all completed work orders for the equipment?

F. Are the equipment manufacturer's recommendations for PM kept on file for reference?

G. Are all significant equipment failures analyzed to determine cause of failure and to recommend a solution?

H. Do the PM check sheets include manufacturer's recommendations as well as points from the historical records?

I. Are advanced diagnostic techniques and equipment used?

J. Are PM work orders generated by a tickler file, card, or a computer system?

K. Is there a fail-safe system to prevent missed inspections?

L. Are all PM and lubrication routes preestablished?

M. Are the PM expenses part of the budget?

N. Are the requirements for the PM program reviewed at least annually to determine the need for changes or adjustments?

11. Engineering

A. Is reliability engineering used to control downtime?

B. What percentage of equipment is analyzed to determine:

1. Mean time between failures
2. Mean time to repair.

C. What percentage of the equipment is covered by a scheduled diagnostic routine?

D. Are all engineering drawings kept up to date and complete?

E. Is maintenance input considered when a new layout is being made?

F. Is maintenance included in any reviews of new equipment purchase considerations?

G. Is maintenance included in any spares standardization programs?

H. Are engineering drawings and specifications made promptly available to maintenance as updates are made?

I. Does maintenance work with engineering on part acquisition for all major overhauls and rebuilds?

12. Work Measurement

A. How are maintenance time standards set?

1. Predetermined times?
2. Standard data?
3. Direct measurement?
4. Work sampling?
5. Estimates?
6. Past history?

B. What application system is used?

1. Slotting and work comparison?
2. Direct comparison?
3. None?

C. What percentage of actual hours worked is covered by a standard?

D. Is there a wage percentage plan tied to output or performance?

E. Is work sampling performed at regular intervals to determine worker productivity and reasons for work delays?

F. Are work sampling results used to improve the maintenance program?

G. Are the schedules for maintenance work based on realistic standards considering the performance standards?

H. Is there a monthly or weekly performance report by
craft based on the work standards?

I. Are all breaks kept to a minimum (15 minutes)?

J. Does productive work time start within 15 minutes of
starting time and end within 15 minutes of quitting
time?

K. Is one worker used per assignment unless safety or job
activity requires more craftworkers?

13. Data Processing

A. Does the maintenance system include any computer
support?

B. Which information is on the computer system?

C. Is the system real-time or batch-processing?

Maintenance Analysis—
Part 3: Organizational Attitudes

A fully developed maintenance management organization requires an understanding of some of the basic responsibilities of
management. Four general responsibilities are to:

1. establish the purpose of the organization;
2. determine measurable objectives to support the purpose;
3. set a permissible variance for the objectives; and
4. determine the actions necessary to maintain the organization within the variance.

These very general statements must be applied to maintenance—the last opportunity some organizations will have to
achieve their "World Class" programs. For example, how can
Just-In-Time, Total Quality Control, or Total Employee Involvement programs work with unreliable or poorly maintained
equipment? Consider the following examples.

How can Just-In-Time programs work with equipment availability of 60%? Current management philosophy is to buy

enough equipment to assure sufficient capacity to support the Just-In-Time program. However, what would happen if we maintained the equipment to assure 100% availability? What would the savings be in capital investment? More than the maintenance cost would be to assure 100% availability! But which course do organizations choose? Examine a good cross section of organizations in this country, and you will see an excess of redundant equipment, and thus unnecessary capital expenditures.

What about Total Quality Control programs? How many of the Quality Circles contain skilled members of the maintenance staff? In cases where companies do include maintenance as part of the team, they fail to use maintenance to provide them with any competitive advantage. Consider this question: what percentage of all your organization's quality problems is related to maintenance? 20%? 50%? Even more? How can U.S. companies expect to compete in a world market that already recognizes the valuable contribution maintenance can make to their competitive efforts. If U.S. organizations don't use this tool in their efforts to improve quality, they will be at a major disadvantage.

How about the maintenance effect on Total Employee Involvement? What is an employee's attitude when he or she recognizes a problem that management refuses to see, much less act on? As taught by any T.E.I. expert or consultant, when management refuses to recognize or correct a problem, it leads to ineffectiveness of the program. Many problems that T.E.I. teams can identify are related to the lack of good maintenance fundamentals. How will these programs eventually end if management refuses to recognize and act on good maintenance fundamentals? The results could be disastrous. Without skilled maintenance technicians to provide answers to equipment-related problems, organizations will lose their competitive edge.

The method to raise management's awareness of the value of maintenance to the organization is to show the value of maintenance in a bottom-line-oriented manner. Using financial information to assist in making maintenance-related decisions is one of the most effective ways to raise organizational awareness. The key is to view maintenance expenditures in the view of "Total Cost."

When examining the cost of a maintenance action, plot it against the costs of nonmaintenance, such as:

* lost production cost
* costs required to make up lost production
* quality costs, particularly rework and scrap energy costs
* customer satisfaction costs
* delayed delivery penalties
* lost customer costs
* environmental penalty costs
* safety penalty costs
* devaluation of capital assets.

It is only when organizations understand the impact of maintenance (the "Total Cost Concept") that the goal to be competitive will be achieved.

Maintenance improvement requires a long-term commitment. The Japanese realize and openly explain that a TPM program takes three to five years of implementation. Organizations in the U.S. will have to be willing to put the same kind of effort into implementation of maintenance improvement programs. Organizational management must realize that PM, PDM, TPM, and CMMS are not part of the program-of-the-month club offerings. Maintenance improvement requires commitment and time to achieve results.

What *is* required is a pathway to develop maintenance improvement programs by raising organizational understanding. A tool developed to help facilitate the communications necessary to achieve this understanding is the Maintenance Management Maturity Grid on pages 36 and 37. This grid was developed from concepts used in the Quality Management Maturity Grid by Phillip Crosby in his book *Quality Is Free* (New York: McGraw-Hill Book Company, 1979).

The grid is divided into stages and categories. The stages are the steps that organizational management progresses through on the path to maturity. When using the grid to evaluate the organization, managers will not miss which stage they are in by more than 1, unless they are using the "ostrich" method of managing. Organizations that have used this grid to evaluate themselves have mailed out copies to various departments. Each department would then circle the stage they felt the organization was at in each category. They compiled the results, and averaged for the organization. They used the total results to build a maintenance improvement program for the organization.

The resulting program is more readily accepted by the organization, since all departments are included and understand the goals. The Maintenance Management Maturity Grid not only helps organizations see their present status, but also clarifies the steps required to reach the next stage as well as the derived benefits.

Categories

There are seven measurement categories, and each addresses a key part of an organization's maintenance program. The responses under each category are typical of the maturity of the organization.

1) Corporate/Plant Management Attitude: This category describes how upper management views the maintenance organization. It is important since no maintenance improvement program will ever succeed without strong management support. Achieving this support will require education about the financial impact maintenance has on the organization. Since upper management understands the factors affecting the bottom line, all communications should be translated into this language.

2) Maintenance Organization Status: This category examines the type of attitude that maintenance uses to approach its work. Many organizations use the "fire-fighting" approach to maintenance. The number of organizations diminish as you move across the grid into the successive categories: this is evident since there are very few organizations practicing productive maintenance in North America.

3) Percentage of Maintenance Resources Wasted: This category relates to the previous one, since the more reactive an organization is, the more resources it wastes. Studies show that reactive organizations waste 30% or more of the controllable maintenance resources. As maintenance disciplines become effective, the wastes are reduced. Good planning and scheduling practices, coupled with effective work order systems, help to eliminate waste.

4) Maintenance Problem Solving: This is the trouble-shooting part of the maintenance organization. Reactive organizations do not use effective problem-solving techniques, since they do not have time. As maintenance becomes more controlled, more time is allocated to cause-and-effect analysis. This allows the maintenance organization to be proactive, not reactive.

5) Maintenance Workers, Qualifications, and Training: One of the largest problems facing maintenance organizations in the 90's is the skill level of the workforce. This problem, coupled with management's lack of commitment to training and inflexibility of the workforce, makes this category one of the most critical on the grid. Close examination of the organization's attitude in this category is extremely important.

6) Maintenance Information and Improvement Actions: This category deals with the maintenance information system, which is the work order. The work order is the key to planning, scheduling, information gathering, communication, etc. The disciplines surrounding the effective use of the work order system spell success or failure for the maintenance improvement plan.

7) Summation of the Company Maintenance Position: This category was included to help organizations find themselves on the grid. Each stage is really a summation of the preceding categories. If a company is reactive and has most of the attitudes of an uncertain organization, then they will not understand why equipment failures occur. They will then do something like fire the maintenance manager, which accomplishes nothing but adding confusion. When looking at this category, an organization should be careful to avoid elevating itself to the highest stage unless all other categories reflect the same level of commitment.

Stages

The stages of organizational development are listed horizontally across the grid. The five stages are distinct enough to provide an organization with the ability to be classified.

1) Uncertainty: Organizations in this category have no understanding of the value of maintenance to their competitive position. Organizations in this stage blame the maintenance organization for equipment problems. The basic problem is a lack of understanding of maintenance and what its real role in the organization should be. However, here is where the problems arise. Everyone knows how maintenance should be done, just ask:

the production manager

engineering

the operations manager

the purchasing manager

the inventory manager

the facility manager

any manager.

The problem is that each of these groups understands how maintenance affects its own area, but cannot see the overall picture of how maintenance affects the entire organization.

Organizations that are in this stage live for today only and have no concept of what the future holds. As long as they can keep the equipment running today, tomorrow will take care of itself. If you ask one, no manager is going to say he or she is like this. However, look at what the company is doing by utilization of the various measurement categories. Is there a disciplined work order system with effective planning and scheduling? Is there a preventive/predictive maintenance program being utilized effectively? Are the maintenance craftworkers multiskilled and cross-trained? Organizations believe that they have enough problems for today, so let the future take care of itself.

2) Awakening: This stage allows an organization to begin realizing what maintenance can contribute; however, it is not yet convinced. The lack of conviction leads to the lack of commitment. The lack of commitment leads to the lack of proper funding.

The difference between uncertain and awakening organizations is that the uncertain ones do not care about what the future holds; awakening organizations do care, and are somewhat aware, but do not want to commit the resources. The results are the same: neither group does anything.

Organizations in this category will talk about long-range plans, predictive maintenance, computerized maintenance systems, and training of the workforce; however, they don't ever take any action. The lack of action is caused by the organization's lack of understanding of maintenance and how it relates to investment spending.

A second problem is the lack of understanding by the maintenance managers in the area of advanced maintenance techniques and technologies. I will always remember one management presentation to an organization that used a prodigious amount of rotating equipment. When the presentation turned to predictive maintenance, the maintenance manager said (in front of his executive directors) that vibration analysis was unproved and had no place in their organization. This organization will never understand or commit to advanced maintenance techniques and technologies if the maintenance professionals do not prepare their upper management.

The culture change for maintenance is more evident in the area of computerized maintenance systems. Many organizations in the awakening stage feel that this is a quick fix to their problems. Unfortunately, they fail to realize that this is a project with an average of approximately 10 months of implementation time and a payback of 15 months. This lack of understanding has contributed to many failed improvement programs.

Organizations will never move out of the awakening category without acquiring a good understanding of maintenance basics.

3) Enlightenment: Organizations moving from awakening to enlightenment do so because of education. These organizations come to clearly understand the value of maintenance. They acquire an understanding of the true costs of maintenance. This involves the understanding of the "Total Costs" concept.

The "Total Costs" concept helps all parts of the organization to communicate. This enhanced communication occurs when everyone understands the financial impact that maintenance decisions have on the bottom line. This leads to considering maintenance as part of the team: operations, engineering, and maintenance work together to solve problems. Finger-pointing decreases and team work increases.

Management of the enlightened organization recognizes the value of a workforce skilled in advanced maintenance technologies and techniques. The management commitment necessary to achieve this level of workforce development begins to convince the unbelievers in the organization, so that the workforce no longer feels that management is "trying to put one over on them." They feel the commitment and respond with their own personal commitment. The organization is making progress.

4) Wisdom: At this stage, an organization realizes the benefits achieved during the stage of enlightenment, and works hard to keep the organizational support necessary to make further progress. This stage requires benchmarking and progress reports. The quickest way to fall back a stage or two is to lose organizational support for the maintenance improvement program.

Organizations in this category do not think they have arrived, because they know that continuous improvement must be made. The comment was once made that "when you think you have arrived, it is time for the organization to replace you with someone who has better vision." This is the attitude of those in the Wisdom stage. The World Class theme of "Continuous and Rapid Improvement" is the charter of the organization in this stage.

Maintenance organizations in this stage do not get sidetracked. They know that the way they can contribute to a World Class organization is to help achieve the three goals:

The Maintenance Organizational Maturity Grid

Measurement Category	Stage 1 Uncertainty	Stage 2 Awakening	Stage 3 Enlightenment	Stage 4 Wisdom	Stage 5 Certainty
Corporate/Plant Management Attitude	No comprehension of maintenance prevention; fix it when it's broken [1]	Recognizes that maintenance could be improved, but is unwilling to fund [2]	Learns more about ROI; becomes more interested and supportive [3]	Participative attitude; recognizes management support is mandatory [4]	Includes maintenance as a part of the total company system [5]
Maintenance Organization Status	REACTIVE: Works on equipment when it fails; otherwise very little productivity [1]	CONSCIOUS: Still reactive but rebuilds major components and has spares available when failures occur [2]	PREVENTIVE: Uses routine inspections, lubrication, adjustments, and minor service to improve equipment M.T.B.F. [3]	PREDICTIVE: Utilizes techniques such as vibration analysis, thermography, N.D.T., sonics, etc. to monitor equipment condition, allowing for proactive replacement and problem solving instead of failures [4]	PRODUCTIVE: Combines prior techniques with operator involvement to free maintenance technicians to concentrate on repair data analysis and major maintenance activities [5]
Percentage (%) of Maintenance Resources Wasted	30+% [1]	20–30% [2]	10–20% [3]	5–10% [4]	Less than 5% [5]
Maintenance Problem Solving	Problems fought as they are discovered [1]	Short-range fixes are provided; elementary failure analysis begins [2]	Problems solved by input from maintenance, operations, and engineering [3]	Problems are anticipated; strong team problem-solving disciplines are utilized [4]	Problems are prevented [5]

	[1]	[2]	[3]	[4]	[5]
Maintenance Workers, Qualification and Training	Poor work quality accepted; rigid craft lines; skills outdated; skills training viewed as unnecessary expense; time in grade pay; low worker turnover/apathy	Workers' lack of skills linked to breakdowns; trade/craft lines questioned; skills obsolescence identified; training needs recognized; traditional pay questioned	Quality + Quality = Quality; expanded/shared job roles; a few "critical skills" developed; training expenses reimbursed; new pay level for targeted skills; increased turnover/fear of change	Quality work expected; "multiskill" job roles; skills up to date and tracked; training required and provided; pay for competency progression	Pride and professionalism permeate; work assignment flexibility; skilled for future needs; operators trained by maintenance, ongoing training; percent of pay based on plant productivity; low employee turnover/high enthusiasm
Maintenance information and Improvement Actions	Maintenance tries to keep records, disciplines are not enforced, poor data	A manual or computerized work order system is used by maintenance; little or no planning or scheduling	A manual or computerized work order system is used by maintenance, operations, engineering; planners used; scheduling enforced	A computerized maintenance control system is used by all parts of the company; information is reliable and accurate	A maintenance information system is integrated into the corporate operation
Summation of Company Maintenance Position	"We don't know why the equipment breaks down; that is what we pay maintenance for. Sure, our scrap rates are high, but that's not a maintenance problem."	"Do our competitors have these kinds of problems with their equipment? Scrap is costing us a bundle!"	"With the new commitment from management, we can begin to identify and solve problems."	"Everyone is committed to quality maintenance as a routine part of our operational philosophy. We can't make quality products with poorly maintained equipment."	"We don't expect breakdowns and are surprised when they occur; maintenance contributes to the bottom line!"

1. the highest quality product or service,
2. at the lowest possible cost, and
3. the best on-time delivery.

5) Certainty: Certainty is the stage of maintenance management maturity. This will involve "World Class" programs such as TPM, advanced preventive/predictive technologies, highly trained and efficient workforces, and advanced use of computerized systems. The organizations in this category have also learned another important lesson: if you don't expect maintenance problems, they will not occur. While this may seem to be unrealistic, those companies who have achieved this stage know it to be true. Organizations that are still at uncertainty think this is too expensive and too unrealistic a goal.

Using the Grid

The grid is just another tool for an organization to use to improve maintenance. It accomplishes a basic task: it allows the various parts of an organization to agree on their present status of maintenance. Once the present status is agreed upon, the grid accomplishes a second task: it allows an organization to plan the future, particularly the actions necessary to improve maintenance.

The third task of the grid is to provide a reflection on the past. Organizations that are making progress have only to look back a stage or two and remember how things used to be. This is often enough incentive to make them push ahead for the next stage.

Since maintenance is a support function, it should be noted that its status is fluid. Reorganization, or a management change, may move the company back a stage or two; but by using the same method to make the initial progress—education—these steps can quickly be regained.

The process of maintenance improvement is important to organizations wanting to survive the competitive 90's. It is hoped that the Maintenance Management Maturity Grid can be of some value to your organization in achieving this goal.

An Introduction
to Maintenance
Management
Systems

An Introduction to Maintenance Management Systems

In computerizing maintenance, there are certain concepts that must be understood and adhered to by the organization. One of the most overlooked is maintenance planning.

Maintenance Planning

Management surveys show that the average productivity of maintenance employees is between 25 and 35%. This means that a craftsman has less than 4 hours of productive time per 8–hour day due to poor maintenance management.

Maintenance employees, whether craftsmen or supervisors, readily recognize the symptoms of a lack of maintenance management procedures, with the result that craftsmen are forced to wait, which means they are spending time unproductively.

The following are some of the most common wastes of productive time.

Multiple trips to stores for materials.

Return trips for tools to do the job.

Trips to the job site to see what is required.

Parts not in stock; wait for delivery from vendor.

Incomplete planning and communication.

Poor craft coordination.

Waiting for drawings from engineering.

Looking for supervisor to get instructions or answers to questions.

Waiting for next work assignment for the next job.

Insufficient workers scheduled for job.

Waiting for equipment to be shut down.

Being pulled off job because of emergency work.

On the average, 2 hours are lost every time a worker is pulled off a job for any reason. To prevent this major loss of productivity, it is necessary to implement some form of job planning function. Planning can be accomplished by the supervisor if there are relatively few maintenance personnel. If there are more than 20 craftsmen, planning is best done by separate maintenance planners, otherwise the foremen have a tendency to do paperwork when they could more profitably spend their time in supervising and directing the work of the craftsmen.

The concept of job planning is to determine what is to be done and how it is to be done. Job planning consists of two main areas: craft skills and materials required for the job. These labor and material requirements may be converted into dollars to give an estimate of the cost of completing the work order.

The importance of planning cannot be overemphasized. Planning is to maintenance what production control is to production. In production, labor measurement is impossible without knowing how, where, and when the work is to be done. Work measurement in maintenance is impossible unless the how, where, and when questions are also answered.

A clear indicator of the importance of planning to CMMS is the *Engineer's Digest* and AIPE (American Institute of Plant Engineer's) Survey (1992), which showed that of those companies having a maintenance planner, 91% were also computerized. Planners are essential functional positions for CMMS success.

(*Note:* The following concepts are presented in general terms. It is widely recognized that no two maintenance organizations are alike—what works for one may not work for another. These concepts may be adjusted or customized for use in different organizations.)

Types of Work to be Planned

Emergency maintenance and critical maintenance (work needed immediately or within 24 hours) is seldom planned. These requests are of short duration and are performed so quickly that there is no time to plan them. These types of work orders should not be considered in the planning functions.

Normal corrective or routine work orders should be the primary consideration of the planning function. These work orders are received and placed in the work backlog. As the workforce and materials become available to carry out the work, it is scheduled. Included in this type of work are preventive and predictive maintenance work orders.

The other group of work requests that can be planned are the shutdown, turnaround, or the outage work orders. For this type of work, it is important that the equipment be shut down and overhauled in the shortest possible time. Only by accurate estimating and scheduling of these work requests can the shutdown be successful.

How to Plan Maintenance Work

Effective planning requires the planners to be skilled and knowledgeable in the craft area they are planning; therefore, supervisors or top craftsmen will make the best planners. If an inexperienced individual is promoted to planner, the results of the planning program will not be satisfactory. Instead of increasing productivity, you may find productivity decreasing.

The planning begins once the work order is approved by management. It is then assigned to the planner, who carefully studies the job. The planner must then decide the following:

1. the crafts required,
2. the time required,
3. the materials required, and
4. whether outside help in the form of specialists, contractors, or special rental equipment is required.

When the planner is deciding on the required crafts, he or she must also decide not only the number of craftsmen and the number of crafts, but also the skill level of the craftsmen. Where journeymen may be required for one assignment, apprentices may be able to complete the other assignments.

The time estimate for the work order is important. If there is no time estimate, you will never know the man-hours of work that is in the craft backlog. Without this information, you can never accurately determine the proper staffing levels for your plant.

The materials required for the work order will determine whether it can be scheduled. If the necessary materials are not available and the work order is scheduled, the craftsmen will lose productivity looking for the parts and waiting for the supervisor to find them work that can be performed. It is also necessary to plan the materials so that an accurate estimate of the cost of the work order can be obtained.

The miscellaneous items to be planned are important to proper completion of the work order. If special skills are required from an outside source, the in-house craftsmen may not be able to complete the work order quickly or with the necessary quality. Also, if special tools or equipment are required, it would be pointless to schedule the work order without them. Trying to jury-rig the hob generally results in lost productivity.

Once the work order is planned and scheduled, the planner should be available in case questions arise on procedure or materials for the work order.

Job Estimating and Scheduling Techniques

When the planner estimates the labor requirements for the work order, there are a few useful tools he or she can rely on to make accurate estimates. There are three methods that may be used:

1. timeslots,
2. universal time standards, and
3. time study estimates.

Timeslots: One of the most accurate approaches to maintenance scheduling is timeslots. Manually, it requires calculations to be performed. Some computerized systems, discussed later, will automatically calculate the timeslots.

In the timeslot method, work orders are not estimated as an hourly quantity, but as an "*A*" job, "*B*" job, "*C*" job, etc., for the particular craft. An *A* job may be 0–2 hours, a *B* job 2–4 hours, etc., depending on the timeslots for the particular shop.

The timeslots may also be judged and bounded by "benchmark jobs" that everyone is familiar with. Thus, an *A* job may be "harder than changing contractor tips but easier than changing a movable arm;" a *B* job may be "harder than changing a movable arm but easier than changing a contractor;" etc.

In estimating maintenance work, especially when it is non-repetitive, it is far easier to "hit" a wide timeslot accurately than a single time value. Timeslots provide the following information: job-estimating standards for every job and craft; and accurate workload estimates for planners.

If the planner estimates the job as an *A* job (e.g., electrical work), then the average length of time to complete an *A* job must be figured into the estimate. It is not expected that every job will take the average length of time; but if there are 10 *A* jobs, it is safe to estimate that they will take about 10 times the average for an *A* job, which will equal the total number of hours in the craft backlog. For example, if $A = 1.5$ hours, then $10 \times 1.5 = 15$ hours in the craft backlog for the *A* jobs. The timeslot method allows accurate total workload estimates by craft, and therefore enables accurate workload scheduling.

In order to be accurate, the timeslot estimates should be recalculated every week, using the last 20 weeks' average, for the completed work orders. While this may result in a lot of paperwork, a computerized system can do this automatically.

Universal Time Standards: Universal time standards are a compilation of the average time it take to perform standard jobs in industry. They are very similar to the auto repair estimate manuals used in garages. They give the average time it will take to perform standard jobs. While these are good benchmarks, they can lead to frustration for the supervisors and the craftsmen. Since maintenance is somewhat unique for each plant, the estimates may not be totally accurate for the site. Also, these standards can be used only when the exact conditions for the estimate are met.

If the universal time standards are used, they should only be used as guides, not for exact scheduling. If the planner can learn to use them, compensating for variations in types of equipment, tools, or environmental conditions, they can be a useful tool. As was true of the timeslot, there are computerized systems that make use of the universal time standards.

Time Study Standards: If this method is to be used, it will require a comprehensive time study to develop the standards. The time study involves the observance of the actual jobs, timing them while performed, and noting the job conditions. While this takes considerable time and effort, the results will be accurate and customized to your installation. However, the cost, training required, and the length of implementation time are major drawbacks to beginning the project. It is beyond the scope of this text to deal with the process used to develop these estimates. Most industrial engineering texts will provide the necessary information for the project.

Estimating Jobs: This method is merely the estimate of how long the job will take. In most cases, it is the "best guess" method. However, if the planner has job experience, it is possible to be accurate most of the time. This method is the least costly way of establishing standards and can be used for planning and scheduling and, to some measure, as a yardstick for efficiency.

The disadvantages include the accuracy of the planner. If the planner is working new jobs, i.e., jobs having no previous estimations or jobs using new methods or tools, then the estimate is just a guess. Also, the estimations can affect the morale of the workers, so that they do not use the estimation as a goal. The most damaging disadvantage is that when the planner quits, you lose much of the data that went into planning the work. A documented method of planning is preferred.

Gross Versus Net Capacity

Another area where problems develop during scheduling is the number of hours to schedule for the week. The question is: do you schedule to your gross capacity or your net capacity? The difference between gross capacity and net capacity might best be illustrated by a paycheck. Most paychecks show the gross amount earned for the pay period. However, what you can spend is the net amount, which is what is left after taxes, FICA, and any other deductions.

The same is true with maintenance scheduling. You have a gross amount of hours to schedule, which is the number of employees times the number of hours scheduled for the week. You may add to this the hours worked by outside contractors and scheduled overtime for the workforce.

To arrive at the net capacity, you should subtract from the gross capacity the following:

1. average emergency work for the week,
2. average preventive hours, and
3. average standing work orders.

This leaves you with the net capacity of hours to schedule. If you schedule more than this amount, you should not expect to get it done. If you do, it is because you are having lower than average hours in one of the three areas above. However, scheduling beyond your net capacity is a source of frustration to the supervisors and the craftsmen. Also, it can lower your credibility with management for promising something you cannot deliver.

Maintenance Work Orders

Before computerization of a maintenance organization can begin, there is a need to set up a method of collecting the information, as discussed in the first chapter. The basic device used to enable a maintenance organization to collect and organize this information is the work order. The work request is a form that is used to initiate a request for maintenance work. Once the work request is approved, it becomes the work order. The work order should produce information on the following:

* maintenance performance

* maintenance costs

* equipment history.

By careful utilization of this information, the maintenance organization should be able to issue maintenance budget forecasts allowing the various areas serviced to plan for the necessary maintenance expenditures.

In addition to the preceding objectives, the work order should also be capable of providing the following:

* a method for requesting maintenance services

* a method for recording maintenance tasks and their start and completion dates

* a method of identifying the type of work to be performed

* a method of providing detailed instructions for each step of the job to be performed

* a method of authorizing work when the costs will exceed a certain level

* a method of planning and scheduling the work

* a method of assigning the work to the craftsmen

* a method of recording the use of special tools and materials

* a method of recording labor and materials costs

* a method of generating reports that can measure labor and supervision efficiency

✳ a method of generating reports that allow for cost analysis of all maintenance tasks.

Work Order Number

The key to the success of a work order system is the work order number. This number identifies the specific maintenance request. All maintenance charges (labor, materials, etc.) are identified by this number. To properly utilize the work order, a number must be assigned to each work request. This is for any work, whether planned, unplanned, emergency, or preventive maintenance.

Planned work is work requested that can be planned, scheduled, and completed without causing delays to the operations. Unplanned work is work requested that is of short duration and that may be performed by a craftsman while working on another task in the same area. This work may be of a critical nature that will quickly lead to an emergency if corrective action is not taken. Emergency work requests (also called breakdown orders) are requests for work due to equipment breakdowns or pending breakdowns. There may not be time to fill out a work order before the work is started. However, to make the system work properly, the work request should be filled out at the first opportunity. This will still allow for all related costs to be charged to the work order number.

Preventive maintenance work orders fall into the same class as planned work orders. They should still be recorded separately so that the preventive maintenance (PM) costs can be accurately tracked. Preventive maintenance tasks are assigned standing or repetitive work order numbers. This will allow the tracking of all charges made to a certain PM task. This will help in determining the cost effectiveness of the PM program. Repetitive tasks that are not PM tasks, but are performed on a periodic basis, should also be assigned standing or repetitive work order numbers. This system will allow the manager to track the work order costs for specific tasks, assuring that excessive time is not spent on certain tasks.

Work Order Forms

Once the numbering system is devised, the work order form must be considered. The maintenance department may choose to use forms that are supplied by certain vendors, or may choose to make up its own forms and have them printed. Whichever is chosen, the following are points to consider when selecting a work order form.

Work Request Definitions

The work order form should provide for the individual work order number. The forms may be preprinted with a sequential number on each form. The form should also provide a means for entering the equipment number (identifying where the work is being performed) for tracking the maintenance costs. For accounting purposes, the report should provide a space for entering an accounting or project number.

In further specifying the work request, the work order should include:

* priority rating
* the type of work to be performed
* a description of the work requested.

In some installations, the priority and type of work are coded; that is, a list of the possible priorities and work types is made up and codes are assigned. To keep the records consistent, each work request is then assigned a priority code and a work class code, identifying the importance of the work and the type of work to be performed.

Work Order Scheduling

To allow for proper scheduling of the work request, there should be some place on the work order for the supervisor (or, in some installations, a planner) to estimate the following requirements to perform the work: the man-hours, the crafts, and the materials. This will assist in proper scheduling of the work order.

In figuring costs, there should be some method of entering planned costs by the requester. In some cases, the work order form may need a space for an individual to approve the work request if the total cost is to exceed some predetermined level.

The work order form should also allow for detailed instructions concerning the work order to be entered. This would include the job plan (the instructions on how to carry out the work request).

Report Information

The work order form should also allow space for the entry of the actual material and labor charges. This can be compared to the estimates, after the completion of the work order, in order to determine efficiency.

The work order form should also allow space for the entry of the description of the actual work performed. This, when compared to the work planned, will help rate the efficiency of the planning. Also, there can be work codes specifying the work that was performed to shorten the time required in filling out the completed work order.

Using Work Order Forms

In practice, the following scenario is typical in processing a work order.

Step 1: The work order is received by the maintenance department. The work order request is entered on a work order form with a number preassigned to it. This number will be the key to the work order's progress through the system. Where multiple copies of the work order are used, the number should be clearly imprinted on each copy.

Step 2: The individual requesting the work should be identified on the work order.

Step 3: The equipment the work is being requested on, and the reason for the request, should be entered on the work order.

Step 4: A detailed but brief description of the work requested should be entered on the work order. It should be noted that to save space on the form, the above information can be coded. The following are some of the fields that can be coded:

* authorizer

* supervisor

* type of work

* status

* equipment.

Step 5: The requester assigns the work order a priority, according to the standard procedures for the particular installation.

Step 6: The requester enters the date of the request and the desired completion date. The requester will then keep one copy and forward the other(s) to the maintenance department.

Step 7: The planner (the individual planning the work order) will review the work order request. If the planner is in agreement with the requester's input, the work order planning will begin. If the planner is not in agreement, then the requester should be contacted and the necessary changes agreed on.

Step 8: Once authorization is given to perform the work, the planner begins to schedule the job. Once the planner is assured that the labor, parts, materials, and equipment are ready, the work order can be scheduled.

If the work order is not to be scheduled at present, it is placed in the work backlog. The backlog is a master file of all incompleted work orders.

Step 9: When the work order is scheduled, the maintenance supervisor in charge of the work will be given a copy of the work order. The supervisor will arrange any last-minute details necessary for the work to begin.

Step 10: The supervisor assigns the craftsmen to the work order. Upon completion of the work order, the craftsmen report the following information:

* materials used

* hours worked

* description of the actual work performed.

Step 11: The supervisor verifies the information on the work order and returns it to the maintenance planner.

Step 12: The maintenance planner then completes the information on the work order. After the necessary information is provided, the work order is filed in the equipment history record.

Usage of Completed Work Order Information

The information on completed work orders can be used to track maintenance costs for equipment and department expenses. The two main types of expenses that can be tracked are labor and material charges.

Labor charges are taken from the work order time charges as reported by the craftsmen and supervisors. The time charges entered are recorded as expenses against the work order. The time charges can also be used to enter the payroll information for each employee, assuring that all time is accounted for.

Material charges are taken from the material information entered on the work order by the craftsmen or supervisor. The materials from the stores, including specific spares for the equipment, are recorded. Typical information would include the description of the material used, the part number, and the cost information (this may be filled in by the supervisor or planner). This will allow for timely reordering of critical spares. Space may be allocated for recording any special tools or equipment that the work order required.

How much information management is going to require will determine the size and detail of the work order form. A successful system will allow management to obtain the information needed to analyze costs by:

* the job

* equipment

* crafts

* priorities

* departments.

The backlog of work orders can also be used to determine staffing requirements and equipment shutdown periods.

It must be kept in mind that a work order system is only as good as the personnel using it. If the personnel do not enter accurate information or are not trained in the proper use of record keeping, the system will not function properly or efficiently. By the use of skilled personnel, particularly in the planning and scheduling function, the maintenance department will operate more efficiently. Proper, realistic, and intelligent planning can result in the maintenance workforce performing 80–90% scheduled jobs and only 10–20% emergency (breakdown) or fill-in jobs. Proper use of the feedback information available by using a work order system will help management upgrade and streamline the maintenance function as necessary.

Computerization of Manual Systems

Computerization of a maintenance work order system enhances and improves maintenance efficiency if the correct computerized system for the installation is used. It must be noted that the computerized maintenance management system installation is more effective if there is a manual work order system already in effect. Again, the objectives of the computerized system are as follows.

1. Maintenance of existing equipment

    A. Reducing equipment downtime.
    B. Maximizing the operating life of the equipment.

2. Inspection and service of the equipment

    A. Execution of the PM work within the constraints of production schedules.

3. Installation of the equipment or major refurbishing.

4. Maintenance storekeeping

    A. Minimizing the spare parts inventory.

5. Craft administration

    A. Maximizing the productivity of the workforce.

In order to achieve these objectives, a maintenance manager will require a substantial amount of timely information. In a manual system, this information must be collected by a group of clerks or supervisors using a variety of reporting mediums. The volume and the variety of the information are enough to overwhelm the staff, and soon the process deteriorates.

A well-designed and well-developed computerized system will eliminate the need for most manual paper shuffling, and will minimize the information required by any one individual. Also, all the information provided by the computerized system is available to all individuals in the maintenance function, including the manager, supervisor, planner, store personnel, and accounting.

In larger installations, the computerized system is more effective if it is introduced in stages, rather than instituting the entire program at one time. However, smaller installations may be able to institute a program without producing an information overload. Small systems can be cost effective for departments with as few as five craft employees.

The database required to operate the computerized maintenance department system is developed by input from the maintenance staff. They must identify the equipment to maintain and the parts necessary to maintain them. Since this information is input into the computerized database, it is available to all users of the maintenance management system.

The benefits of computerization include increasing the efficiency of the maintenance department and the production equipment. The largest cost savings are:

    increased craft productivity

    increased equipment uptime

    reduction in stores inventory

    reduction in emergency and critical maintenance.

The accurate filing and recall abilities of the computer allow for more accurate estimations of required labor and materials for the maintenance work orders. More accurate planning and scheduling of the work orders results in a reduction of idle time for craftworkers. Accurate parts inventory and usage allows for the proper inventory levels for stores materials and elimination of unnecessary items.

Quick access to the information in the computer's database makes the supervisors of both the maintenance and production areas aware of the progress of certain work orders. With the filing system for work orders in the backlog, all work order trends can be monitored and controlled. Quick access to this information allows for proper employment levels for each craft to be maintained. The backlog will also help manage the outside maintenance contractors in a cost-effective manner.

Manual record systems make it time consuming to prepare various reports necessary to properly manage a maintenance organization. The computer system, with its almost instantaneous recall, makes report preparation a rapid procedure. The reports from most computerized maintenance management systems include:

* use of employees

* use of stores materials

* costs for maintenance of equipment.

Initially, the preventive maintenance schedules are based on manufacturer's recommendations and industry standards. The computer will automatically schedule the work, and the results can be input into the system. Over a period of time, patterns in wear and failures will develop. By monitoring the reports, improved preventive maintenance plans can be formulated. By monitoring equipment costs, over-maintenance and under-maintenance—both wastes of resources—can be eliminated.

However, to successfully select and use the computerized maintenance management systems, it will be necessary for those involved to have a basic understanding of basic computer technology. This will be provided in the following section.

Computer Systems

In the early days of computer use in maintenance management, only engineers with computer knowledge were able to properly utilize the computer. With the advancements made in computer technology, off-the-shelf computer hardware and software can be purchased and put to work by managers not having special programming skills. As the technology continues to increase, the prices of very powerful systems continue to decrease. There are two main types of computer systems that are presently in use with computerized maintenance management systems:

* mainframe or minicomputers

* microcomputers or PC's.

Mainframe computers are larger, more expensive computers that can be accessed by several users at the same time. This type of computer is usually installed in a room or restricted area not accessed by the users. The users gain access to the computer by remote terminals that are connected to the computer across the telephone lines. Most computer terminals look like microcomputers, having a keyboard and a video display.

Microcomputers (also called personal computers) are designed to be used by only one person at a time unless they are networked. When networked, the PC's have almost the same power as a mini- or mainframe when properly configured. There are numerous such systems on the market, ranging from pocket to desktop size. The typical desktop microcomputer has four components:

* keyboard

* video display

* central processing unit (CPU)

* hard disk for data storage.

The system may also contain one or two disk drives for additional data storage.

Hardware Description

The two units that make up the CPU are the processing unit and the primary memory. The systems component usually contains one or more disk drives for storing the computer programs and data. The computer keyboard is used to transfer the information from the CPU to the disk drive(s). The CPU can receive, store, manipulate, and transfer information. The CPU operates according to the program installed by the manufacturer. This program supervises the flow of data to and from the CPU and other devices in the computer system. This program is part of the microprocessor and cannot be changed by the user.

Instructions and data are stored in the computer in two types of memory chips—ROM and RAM. ROM (read only memory) are programmed by the manufacturer and are used to start up the system and provide the guidelines for the computer operation. The ROM program cannot be changed by the user.

RAM (random access memory) stores the information and programs entered by the users. This is like a giant file cabinet with the memory being divided into thousands of compartments, each with a label (called an address) for storing information. The information is entered in a series of binary digits called bits. A series of eight bits is called a byte. Most microprocessors have 2 to 4 megabytes of RAM. Some microprocessors can be expanded to 32 megabytes or more by adding memory chips.

The cost of the microcomputer can cover a broad spectrum. Some very fine systems begin at $2000 and can go as high as $15,000, depending on the manufacturer. System costs can go higher depending on the peripheral equipment required.

Peripheral Equipment

By itself, the CPU cannot give the user any feedback. The peripheral equipment makes the CPU useful to the user.

MONITOR OR CRT

The first of the peripheral devices is the monitor. The monitor displays the information in a textual form that the user can read. The monitors can be monochrome (display of one color) or color. The price of monochrome monitors begins at $150 and can go as high as several thousand dollars for special high-resolution screens.

Color monitors have been improved to supply sufficient resolution for text displays. Also, for some graphics displays, the color monitors add meaning and emphasis. If higher resolution is needed in color monitors, high-resolution monitors (VGA or SVGA) are available at an increased cost. Basic low-resolution color monitors are available beginning at $200. High-resolution color monitors may run in the $2000–$5000 range.

A new addition to the monitor field is the touch-sensitive screen. This allows the user to touch certain areas of the screen to record input or give commands. The application of this technology has been made in the CMMS market to facilitate the quick entry of information into the computer system.

PRINTERS AND PLOTTERS

Printers are the devices that will provide the user with a print-out (also called hard copy) of the desired records and reports. The two most popular printer styles are dot matrix and laser.

The dot matrix printer uses a printer head made up of tiny wires. These tiny dots are used to make up a particular letter or number. The printer program determines the pattern of the dots for each letter. The different styles of type that may be used are selected by the software program. The advantage of a dot matrix is that it is very fast, and these printers can also produce graphic printouts. The disadvantage is that the quality of print is unsatisfactory for some applications requiring typewriter-quality print. The cost for this type of printer may run from $200 to $2000.

Laser printers are used for higher quality output. They are typically utilized for management reports or graphics requiring presentation quality output. They have hardware similar to copiers, i.e., a developing drum and toner cartridge. The speed of the printer is dependent on the particular application, but speeds of 8 pages per minute are not uncommon. The price of these printers may range from $800 to $5000.

There are also thermal printers, ink jet printers, and plotters that may fall into this category; however, they are not widely used in computerized maintenance management applications to date, with the exception of preparing presentations.

MEMORY STORAGE DEVICES

The most common memory storage devices are disk drives. Disk drives use a rotating magnetic disk to store data. The disks come in two basic types—floppy and hard disks.

Floppy disks are driven at a set speed with a magnetic head resting on the disk through an opening in its protective envelope. The information may be recorded on one or both sides of the disk. There are two basic sizes—5¼" and 3½". The 5¼" disks may contain from 150K bytes to 1.2M bytes. The 3½" disks may contain from 720K bytes to 1.2M bytes. These drives may run several hundred dollars each depending on the manufacturer.

Hard disk systems use a fixed hard disk rotating at a certain speed. The recording head floats one or two microns from the surface of the disk to record the data. They are sealed to prevent any contamination from entering the system. They also are small enough to occupy approximately the same space as the floppy disk systems. The hard disk system can store from 40M bytes to over a gigabyte of information. The disadvantage is the cost. The hard disk system may run from $250 on up (to several thousand dollars) depending on the manufacturer of the system and its size.

INPUT DEVICES

The typical input device for a computerized maintenance management system is the keyboard. The keyboard is a typewriter-like device that converts the keystroke into an electronic signal that is sent to the microprocessor. Keyboards are usually contained in the computer package and do not entail additional costs.

Some systems will use a mouse-type device for movement through the system. These devices are particularly useful when utilizing a "Windows" based system.

Some advancements that are being incorporated into the computerized maintenance management systems include bar code readers, light pens, and voice-actuated systems. These devices allow for more rapid input of data into the system. At present, the application of these systems is under development. The bar code readers are the most developed, with most vendors offering simple bar coding for the inventory functions. The next few years will show further development of auxiliary devices for data input.

Applications of Computerized Maintenance Management Systems

In the previous section, we examined a typical manual work order system. An understanding of that type of system is required before implementation of a computerized maintenance management system will be efficient and effective. With this fundamental knowledge, the application to the computer can now be made.

The computerized maintenance management systems basically all function in the same manner. Some will include more detail and use different terminology, but they all will use the work order system. The computer has a major advantage—speed. While manual systems require large files, and are subject to misplaced data and communication problems, the computerized systems are convenient packages. Even the larger systems require a minimum of paperwork, filing, and time. This section will give a broad overview of a typical system and its uses.

Computerized Maintenance Management

All features included in the computerized maintenance management systems are designed to provide the following advantages to the user.

* Improve maintenance efficiency.

* Reduce maintenance costs.

* Reduce equipment downtime by scheduling preventive maintenance.

* Increase the life of equipment.

* Provide historical records to assist in maintenance planning and budgeting.

* Provide maintenance reports in a format that is required by the user.

Plant and equipment maintenance often comprise a large part of a company's budget. Because of high replacement costs of facilities and equipment, the working life of present equipment must be extended as long as possible. To achieve this goal, equipment maintenance must be accurately scheduled and efficiently performed. Necessary records must be kept.

Computerized maintenance management systems are used to track all maintenance costs and equipment repairs. This tracking is accomplished by the monitoring of work orders. By monitoring work order costs and utilizing proper scheduling of the work orders, the repair costs can be monitored. This supplies management with the necessary information to track and plan maintenance budgets.

A second method of cost control is the monitoring of inventory and purchasing. This will track the equipment parts costs to each piece of equipment. This function will also help avoid excessive inventories. The purchasing module will help with vendor selection and monitor shipping time.

Another prime feature of the computerized maintenance management system is the scheduling of the preventive maintenance function. Proper scheduling of preventive maintenance can reduce "overmaintenance" and still increase uptime and extend the life of the facilities and equipment. There are additional costs incurred when the system is installed, however, the total maintenance costs will decrease over a period of time. This overall reduction is shown in Figure 1.

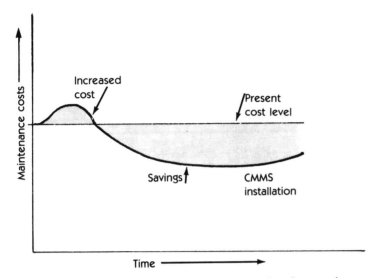

Figure 1. Overall reduction of maintenance costs after the introduction of a computerized maintenance management system (CMMS).

Most computerized maintenance management systems accomplish these objectives through the use of four system modules:

1. work order planning and scheduling
2. maintenance stores controls
3. preventive maintenance
4. maintenance reports.

Each of these functions will be discussed in the following sections.

Work Order Planning and Scheduling

Computerized work orders are documents that detail maintenance work. The computerized work orders should contain information such as:

work order number,

equipment work is requested on,

description of work requested, and

type of work (emergency, routine, PM, etc.) required.

As discussed earlier, the individual work orders provide the documentation necessary to:

* control maintenance performance
* control job and plant costs
* track equipment history.

The basis for an effective work order system is the same as for the manual system—the work order number. All material and labor costs are charged to this number.

Work orders must be input into the system from a maintenance request form, which is filled in by the individual requesting the maintenance work. Once the work order is in the system, the user may look at the work order, update it as it is being worked on, and remove it from the backlog once it has been completed. The work order system flow is shown in Figure 2. The following sections explain the steps used to process work

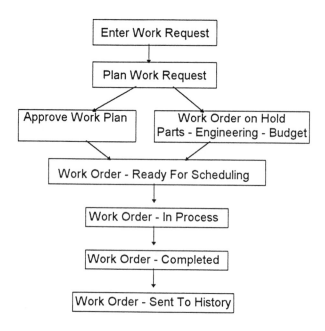

Figure 2. Work Order Flow Diagram

orders in a typical computerized maintenance management system.

The first computerized maintenance management function required is the entering and filing of the work order request information. This process has four main objectives:

1. to provide a means of entering and updating work orders,
2. to provide the ability to inquire into various parts of a work order,
3. to provide a method of charging costs to a work order, and
4. to provide a method of saving the data on a completed work order.

Work Order Entry

Work orders are entered into the system using the work order entry screen. The process is similar to filling out a manual work order. A sample work order screen is pictured in Figure 3.

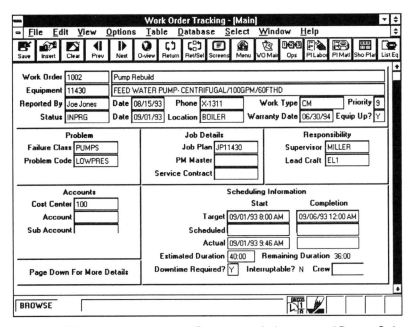

Figure 3. Work order entry screen. (Screen provided courtesy of Project Software and Development Incorporated.)

The user should specify the equipment number of the equipment that requires the maintenance. Other information that should be entered will include the priority and a description of the work required. There may also be a field for estimating the cost of performing the work order. Some work orders will be for complex jobs that will actually require many work orders to be written. When one work order is broken into several smaller work orders for planning and scheduling, these smaller work orders are classified as dependent work orders.

Once a work order is entered into the system, there should be a function to allow for information changes and updates. The information may require changing as the work order becomes defined in more detail. It is possible that more work will be required than previously estimated. Work orders may also require changing if the cost estimates are in error.

There should also be a function to allow the user to look at any information on a given work order. This may be combined with the update function or may be a separate function.

Some work order requests will be broken into smaller dependent work orders. This means that the work requested is large or complex in nature, and must be broken down into several steps or phases. In this case, the program should allow for the display of the dependent work orders. It is usually done by entering the master work order number; the dependent work orders are displayed with a brief description of each work order.

These functions should also display the planned time left to complete each work order.

Work Order Backlog

The backlog is the storage area for all active work orders. As they are entered, the work orders are taken by the computerized maintenance management system and placed in the backlog file. The backlog is the computerized master file of all active work orders.

All work orders entered into the system will remain in the backlog until they are either canceled or completed. Using the backlog, it is possible to look through all active work orders. The backlog search function should also allow the user to select certain work orders by common criteria or characteristics; for example, by equipment number, priority, planner, supervisor, work class, a safety work order status, or whether or not a shutdown is required to work on the work order.

Planning and Scheduling Work Orders

The computerized maintenance management system's work order planning functions provide the information needed to plan work orders. The work order planning function has four objectives:

* to provide an efficient method of requesting and assigning work performed by maintenance personnel,
* to provide an efficient method of transmitting written instructions on the work that is required (and how it is to be done),
* to provide a method of estimating and then recording actual maintenance costs, and
* to provide a method of gathering the information necessary to prepare reports for management.

All work orders will require certain information to ensure that the work is carried out properly. Computerized maintenance management systems provide fields for entering the following information during work order planning:

* labor requirements
* material requirements
* tool requirements
* work order instructions.

The individual planning the work order will be responsible for entering this information on the work order. When the craftsman receives a copy of the work order, the details will ensure that the work is carried out as requested.

Work order planning involves including details on what work needs to be performed, as well as the required labor, tools, and materials. In order for the work order to be scheduled properly and completed on a timely basis, this information is required.

CRAFTS

Work orders will require different crafts, depending on the type of work to be performed. This screen will help the individual doing the planning to schedule the proper crafts for the work order. The following information may be entered:

* craft

* number of craftsmen

* planned hours.

By using the information, the correct number of craftsmen may be scheduled so that the work order is carried out in the most efficient manner.

WORK ORDER INSTRUCTIONS

There will be occasions when a work order becomes so complicated that more information is needed than can be written on the work order. This option can be used to add details. The option can also be used if certain individuals are to be notified when the work begins or reaches a certain point.

MATERIALS

When a work order requires more than just an inspection, it will require materials. It is frustrating to the craftsman to begin a job and find that the required parts are not available. The computerized maintenance management system ensures that the parts are available before the work order is scheduled.

The materials option should provide the following information:

* stock number of required parts

* quantity required

* cost per item

* description of item.

There are several ways this can be done. One is the use of an inventory screen or picklist combination. Some picklists for the inventory may include the option of charging overhead for the materials used.

TOOLS

In planning the work order, it may be noted that some special tools are required to carry out the work. The computerized maintenance management system should allow the individual doing the planning to note the tools required. The information entered includes the following:

* tool ID
* description of the tool
* quantity required
* cost (if necessary).

Entering the above information will prevent the craftsmen from beginning a work order without the proper equipment.

DEPENDENCIES

When one work order depends on another, the dependencies should be noted. This ensures that the necessary work order (or orders) has been performed before the next one is scheduled. For example, it would be difficult to install a component before it has been removed and sent out for repair. It is best to use this type of function if the work order is part of a larger job plan.

Work Order Updates

As conditions change, it is possible that some of the information on the work order plan may require modification. The computerized maintenance management system should provide that option. The change options should include:

* crafts
* work order instructions

* materials

* tools.

Equipment History Inquiry

The computerized maintenance management system should allow the user to look at the history records for any equipment. This information can be used for decisions concerning the equipment.

The records may be accessed all at once or may be broken into three smaller groups. Typical groups are:

* emergency repair history

* PM history

* normal repair history.

By observing the equipment history, repetitive problems can be identified and possible solutions to the problems recommended.

The equipment history inquiry also will help track costs on the equipment. The following costs are samples that could be accumulated:

* labor

* material

* other

* cumulative.

Equipment Parts Catalog Inquiry

This is an essential function for the individual performing the planning. This function should display all of the store stock items listed as parts for a piece of equipment. Once the equipment number is keyed in, the following information should be displayed:

* manufacturer's part number

* part description

* stock number

* quantity used on this piece of equipment.

Scheduling

Work order scheduling utilizes the work orders that are entered into the backlog. The individual doing the scheduling selects the work orders to be scheduled. The scheduler should be able to select the work orders based on any field of information.

The normal process is to place the work order on a ready-to-schedule listing. This is a list of work orders that are ready to be performed. The individual doing the scheduling will daily select the work orders to be scheduled during the next period from the ready-to-schedule listing by date needed and by priority.

If there are spares in the stores, the computerized maintenance management system notifies the user that the spares are available. If the items are not in the stores, the computerized maintenance management system notifies the user that the items are not available and need to be ordered.

Some systems have a feature that daily checks the stores to see if the short items for the work order have been received. If the material has been received, the scheduler is notified by an on-screen message.

WEEKLY SCHEDULES

This feature is used to schedule the work orders for execution by the craftsmen. When placed on the daily schedule, the work order will be printed for distribution.

WORK ORDER COMPLETION

Work order completion will allow the user to complete the displayed work order and remove the completed work order from the active file. The computerized maintenance management system should allow for the actual hours worked. It should also allow for the entry of the various material and labor costs that are charged against the work order. There should also be a space to enter any comments that are required. The system then stores this information for use in the historical and report files.

WORK ORDER COST CHARGES

This function is used to post cost charges against the work order that are not included in the normal labor or material costs. These costs are divided into three areas:

* labor (L)

* material (M)

* other.

Once the charges are entered into the proper field, the computerized maintenance management system will add the charges to the work order for a complete record of expenses.

Labor Records

Time Reporting

This function is used to charge time spent by an employee on a work order to the work order number. The function should allow the input of the employee's identification, the work order number(s) that the employee worked on, and the hourly rate to be paid. This enables the computerized maintenance management system to keep all labor charges debited to the correct work order.

Stores Controls

The stores control module of computerized maintenance management systems is designed to track material costs as they apply to the management function. These modules will help to reduce inventory costs and improve stores accountability. The two primary objectives of the stores control modules are to:

* monitor material status

* manage material sources.

The main stores functions are discussed in the following section.

Material Issue

Store Stock Material Issue

This function is used to update the store stock quantity on hand, and material costs. The stores material, whether planned or unplanned, must be charged to a work order number to properly track costs.

UNPLANNED MATERIALS

Materials are considered unplanned when a work order has been planned and some materials were overlooked in the planned process. It becomes necessary to issue the materials when the work order is scheduled or even being performed. The system should allow for entry of the store item, and it should then be charged against the work order number.

PLANNED MATERIALS

When issuing planned material, the user is releasing the material that was planned for the work order to the employee performing the job.

STOCK RETURN

There are work orders that do not require all of the issued material. When the material is returned to the stores, the system should make it easy to re-enter the information. This function should uptake the stores inventory so that the actual material on hand is accurate.

Store Stock Catalog

To assist the user in determining if a part is in the store stock, the inquiry feature can be used. This allows the user access to the computerized maintenance management system's listing of store stock items. These catalogs may be used in two different methods—alphabetical listing or store stock number.

If the user knows the store stock number of the item, it can be entered and the computerized maintenance management system will list the information for that item. If the

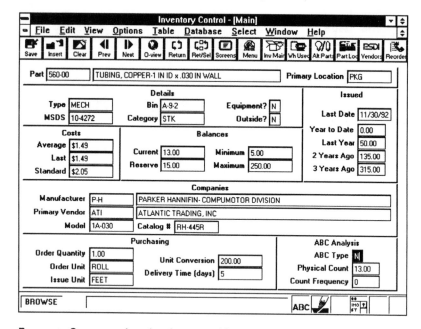

Figure 4. Stores catalog detail screen. (Screen provided courtesy of Project Software and Development Incorporated.)

user doesn't know the stock number, but knows the name of the item, the name can be entered and the computerized maintenance management system will display the required stock information. A typical stores catalog detail screen is pictured in Figure 4.

STOCK ITEM WORK ORDER REFERENCE

This computerized maintenance management system function is used to show what work orders require specific stock material. The function should list:

* a brief description of the work order,

* the amount of material required, and

* the amount reserved for the work order.

To help in ordering the material, the computerized maintenance management system should list the amount of stock on hand, the amount required, and the amount on order. This will allow the user to make logical decisions when placing material orders.

STOCK ITEM—WHERE-USED INQUIRY

This computerized maintenance management system feature shows the equipment where each stock item is used. This allows the user to inquire for any stock item to see where it is used.

STORE STOCK CATALOG INDEX

Each store stock item has a short description. This function allows the user to generate a screen list of all items using the same description, and gives the user access to the store catalog without knowing the stock number. The information should include a description, the stock number, and the quantity on hand. This function is useful in searching for items when the stock number is not known.

STORE STOCK CATALOG—STOCK NUMBER

This function is useful for finding stock items by stock number or partial stock number (if only part of the number is known). The function will list all items with the same stock number or partial stock number.

Store Material Accuracy

Stores Cycle Counts

In order to ensure that the quantity on hand matches the quantity in the computerized maintenance management system, an inventory cycle count is periodically performed. This is a random manual counting of a selected percentage of the stores inventory. Any differences found should be corrected in the computerized maintenance management system to show the actual quantity on hand.

Since only partial amounts of the store stock are counted at any one time, the computerized maintenance management sys-

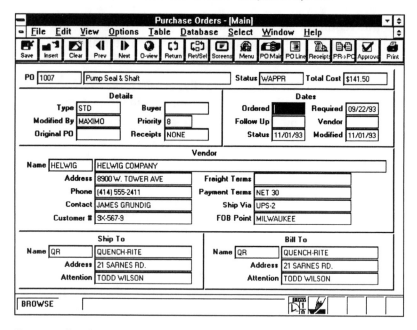

Figure 5. Purchase order screen. (Screen provided courtesy of Project Software and Development Incorporated.)

tem should allow the user to enter how much of the stock is to be counted.

Stock Item Reorder

As the stock amounts of an item are used from the store, it becomes necessary to reorder. This is done by writing a purchase order. The required-by date is important. This date provides a reference for the user to ensure that the material is received in a timely manner. A typical purchase order screen is pictured in Figure 5.

PURCHASE ORDER INQUIRY

Once the purchase orders are written, they are entered into the purchase order backlog. A computerized maintenance management system allows the user to look through the outstanding purchase order. The information should include the amount received and the due date. This allows the user to track partial or late shipments.

As purchase order material is received, it is entered into the system. If partial orders are received, this can also be noted in computerized maintenance management systems. The purchase order will not be closed out until all material is received.

PURCHASE ORDER UPDATE

If there are changes to be made in a purchase order after it has been written, they are made through this computerized maintenance management system function. A typical purchase order detail update screen is pictured in Figure 6.

PURCHASE ORDER MATERIAL RECEIPTS

When materials are ordered on a purchase order, it is necessary to enter them into the stores stock as they arrive. This func-

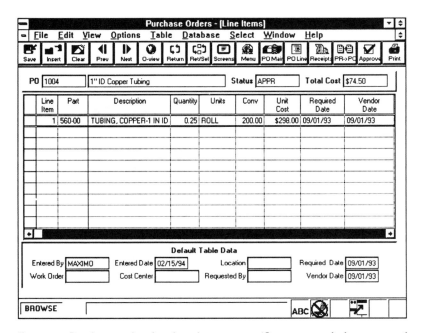

Figure 6. Purchase order detail update screen. (Screen provided courtesy of Project Software and Development Incorporated.)

tion of computerized maintenance management systems allows for material additions to the store stock. It should also allow for entering additional information concerning the shipment and the item. This information includes:

* quantity received
* whether the shipment was partial or complete
* where the material will be located in the store.

This allows for accurate inventory to be kept in the stores, even when frequent purchase order shipments are received.

RETURN TO VENDOR

This function tracks any stock items that are returned to the vendor. This is important in order to receive proper credit for returned items.

Preventive Maintenance

Equipment Preventive Maintenance Entry/Update

This function is used to change or update preventive maintenance scheduling information. A choice is offered to the user: whether the PM is going to be on a calendar schedule or on a schedule determined by meter readings. (Meter readings may be determined by tracking operation time or some other measurable parameter.)

The preventive maintenance module should allow the user to define specific tasks, and group them by craft for each piece of equipment. The module should allow for the entering of the detailed information required to do the tasks. This method provides the craftsmen with enough details to satisfactorily complete the task.

The preventive maintenance tasks should be able to be scheduled by the day, week, month, or quarterly, semiannually, or annually. There should also be areas for estimates of time to complete the task.

When printed, the PM should allow space for the detailed instructions, input from the craftsmen, and room for the craftsmen to show completion and for a supervisor to accept the work.

PM METER READING UPDATE

This function is used to change the meter reading for a piece of equipment, in order to keep it current in the computerized maintenance management system.

PREDICTIVE MAINTENANCE

Some of the more advanced systems are using the meter reading part of the system to monitor given parameters on equipment. These may be vibration, temperature, spectrographic analysis, or chemical levels. Once these readings exceed a certain level, a PM checksheet would be automatically issued, detailing the maintenance action required.

Management Reports

While it is important for management to understand the computerized maintenance management system operation, they will not use most of the features in the system. However, the maintenance-reporting function will provide management with the information necessary to operate the maintenance organization at peak efficiency.

WORK ORDER PRIORITY ANALYSIS

This report lists the number of completed work orders during a specified period of time. The work orders are sorted by area and priority. This will allow monitoring of work order completions to ensure that the work order priorities are being followed.

PLANNER PERFORMANCE

This report is used to monitor planner efficiency. It will show the number of work orders written, number planned, and the planned hours compared to the actual hours it took to complete a work order.

SUPERVISOR WORK ORDER PERFORMANCE

This report compares the supervisor work order actual hours to the planned hours. This will help in the evaluation of the efficiency of the supervisor and work crew.

SUPERVISOR/SKILL WORK ORDER PERFORMANCE

This report compares the planned skill and the actual skill hours for the completed work orders within the selected dates. This will show the efficiency of the supervisor in managing the different skill groups.

WORK ORDER COSTS REPORT

This report lists the costs accumulated for the various work classes within an area. The report will list the costs charged to labor and materials.

COMPLETED WORK ORDER PERFORMANCE

This report lists the planned and actual figures for the following fields:

* total labor hours

* cumulative costs

* labor hours by crafts.

This report allows the evaluation of the work order information by individual work orders that are completed between the start and end dates that are specified.

WORK ORDER BACKLOG SUMMARY

This report will provide a listing of all active work orders in the backlog. The work orders are sorted by priority. This will provide a listing of all work orders that are grouped by what stage they are at in the planning process. This can support the scheduler when looking for work orders that are ready to schedule. It also will show if there are too many work orders waiting to be planned.

EQUIPMENT REPAIR HISTORY

This report lists the equipment repair history for any equipment that has a history. This report will allow analysis of the information in order to spot trends or problems with equipment maintenance.

EQUIPMENT MAINTENANCE COSTS REPORT

This report lists maintenance costs by equipment number. The costs are formatted in two ways:

* costs for the last 12 months
* costs for the month to date.

When this report is selected, all equipment having an equipment maintenance cost history will be printed.

EQUIPMENT MAINTENANCE COST EXCEPTION REPORT

This report lists all equipment (by equipment number) whose costs exceed the monthly estimated budget (also referred to as the cost standard). The report will list the accumulated costs for the last 12 months as well as the costs to date for the month. It also lists the cost standard for comparison.

SAFETY WORK ORDER BACKLOG

This report lists all of the safety work orders in the backlog. The reports are grouped by area, planner, and requested completion date. This will allow monitoring of the safety work orders in the backlog to ensure that they are being completed in a timely fashion.

STOCK ITEM USAGE REPORT

This report will detail the usage of stores material for a given time period. This would include the volume of material used and the total cost. It should also note any items that are at or below the reorder point.

WORK ORDER WAITING REPORT

This report will list all work orders in the backlog that are not ready to schedule. The report should also list the reason why they are not ready to schedule. This will allow those responsible for the work orders to identify their work orders and take appropriate action.

PREVENTIVE MAINTENANCE OVERDUE REPORT

This report will list all of the preventive maintenance orders that are past due. This will assist in preventing any oversight and causing unnecessary damage to the equipment.

REPORT GENERATOR

In many cases, there will be information required that is not gathered by standard system reports. This would require the use of a custom report writer. This is furnished with most CMMS. A sample report generator is pictured in Figure 7.

Selection and Implementation

Do I need a computerized maintenance management system?
After exploring the systems—their advantages and disadvan-

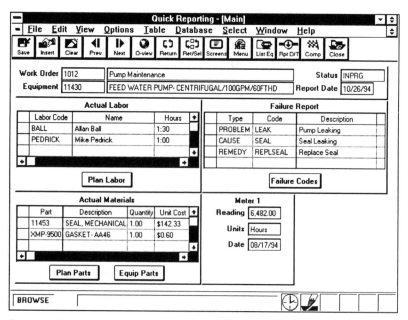

Figure 7. Report generator screen. (Screen provided courtesy of Project Software and Development Incorporated.)

tages—the above question is sure to be raised. There is a three-step process that can be followed to successfully answer that question and others that will result. The steps are:

1. analysis,
2. selection, and
3. implementation.

Analysis

Good planning and control of the maintenance function are derived from the efforts of maintenance supervision. Supervisors must monitor their workforce, see that all necessary records are kept, and ensure that equipment maintenance, including preventive maintenance, is properly scheduled and executed.

However, as the equipment becomes more complex, the industrial facility becomes physically larger, and the number of employees increases, the manager needs help. Increasing the salary workforce may be a temporary solution, but problems will persist. A computerized maintenance management system can help to shrink the problems and complexity of the plant to a manageable level. How does one decide if a computerized maintenance management system is required?

To start, one should examine the present maintenance system. The following are some questions to consider.

1. Are the maintenance costs for your installation rising faster than operation's costs?
2. How much more are you spending on maintenance than you were 5 years ago?
3. Do you know what it costs to maintain each piece of equipment?
4. Do your maintenance craftsmen spend most of their time waiting to work?
5. Do you have storage bins full of spare parts that never seem to be used?
6. Does your equipment seem to break down at the worst possible time without any warning?

7. Do you have access to the information needed to properly plan for the future?
8. Is this information in a usable form?

If these questions call attention to problem areas in your facility, it would be wise for you to investigate computerized maintenance management systems. However, if you feel that the maintenance at your facility is satisfactory, consider the fact that a computerized maintenance management system can help to speed up the present activities. This will not require additional employees—it will increase the productivity of the present workforce. It also will reduce the time required to search for filed information.

To begin, a study needs to be made of the present maintenance organization. This will help to determine how efficient the organization is and where improvements can be made. If it is found to be efficient, consider how efficient the organization will be in five or ten years.

It would be beneficial at this time to take a maintenance audit to see how many problem areas are evident.

(*Note:* A computerized maintenance management system will not improve a poor record keeping system, it will only complicate it.)

System Selection

If the decision is made to investigate a computerized maintenance management system, it is advisable to form a committee. The committee should be made up of individuals from the following areas: engineering, maintenance, stores, accounting, and data processing. This committee should accomplish the following.

* Review present record keeping systems and paper work flow.

* Set objectives of the system in the areas of: work order processing, maintenance stores, preventive maintenance, cost

controls, and required reports (see the next section for further information).

* Identify the type of computer system that the software is to operate on. (If the hardware is to be purchased as well as the software, the decision may be postponed, pending the selection of the software package.)

* Identify the vendor packages that meet the objectives. Some companies with adequate personnel may investigate the possibility of developing their own software. This decision should be made cautiously because it can be a very time-consuming and costly project.

* Evaluate the system and the vendor. This will necessitate contacting the vendor for a meeting where a demonstration can be arranged. In some cases, with smaller systems, the vendor has demonstration programs that can be used to see the system operate. Evaluation of the vendor includes a profile of the vendor, recommendations from clients presently using the system, and the vendor's support capabilities.

* Obtain specific price quotes from each vendor.

This information should then be compiled into a report to management. This report should provide all the necessary information for the selection of the appropriate system. The committee can include a recommendation if there is a system that is better for the application than any others. However, all the evaluated systems should be included in the report.

The following check sheets may be used as a guide to help in the evaluation of a computerized maintenance management system.

Computerized Maintenance Management Check Sheet
Rate for importance: 3 (very) to 0 (not wanted)
Equipment Information

1. Stores equipment information such as cost center, department, location, etc.
2. Allows for cost and repair information to be accessed at multiple equipment levels (e.g., component, subcomponent, assembly, subassembly, etc.)
3. Work orders can be saved to the equipment history as one line of information or full detail.
4. All information in the equipment history can be accessed by sorting on multiple fields of data.
5. The system provides a bill-of-materials for each piece of equipment.
6. The system provides user-defined screens for storing additional information about equipment items/types, which can also be selected and sorted by reports.

Totals for Section   _____

Computerized Maintenance Management Check Sheet
Rate for Importance: 3 (very) to 0 (not wanted)
Preventive Maintenance

1. The system will schedule PM's by the following:
   A. Calendar
   B. Some type of meter reading
   C. Operational parameter (real time)
   D. Combination of any of the above.
2. The system allows for unlimited numbers of PM's per piece of equipment.
3. The system allows for the following amount of text per PM:
   A. One line
   B. Several lines

C. Page(s)
D. Unlimited text.

4. The system allows for multiple crafts to be scheduled on any PM.

5. The system uses the following type of PM schedule:

   A. Fixed (based on fixed frequency)
   B. Sliding (based on last completion date)
   C. Operational parameter demand (interface)
   D. Operational parameter demand (manual entry)
   E. Combination of the above.

6. The system has the ability to schedule PM's for any specific date and/or day of the week.

7. The system has the ability to forecast the following for PM's due for any specified time period:

   A. Labor resources
   B. Material requirements
   C. Special tools.

8. The system will schedule PM's for:

   A. Equipment
   B. Facilities.

9. The system will combine all PM's due for piece of equipment:

   A. Automatically
   B. Manually
   C. Not at all.

10. The system generates the PM work orders:

    A. Daily
    B. Weekly
    C. Monthly
    D. User-defined interval
    E. Other interval.

11. If the system does not produce written PM procedures, it provides a procedure code to locate the list of the tasks to be performed.

12. The system produces a report of the following:

    A. Overdue PM's by the amount overdue
    B. Incomplete PM's
    C. Results of PM inspections.

Totals   _____

Computerized Maintenance Management Check Sheet
Rate for importance: 3 (very) to 0 (not wanted)
Work Orders

---

1. The system tracks the following information at the individual work order level:

    A. Labor planned
    B. Labor actual
    C. Materials planned
    D. Materials actual
    E. Tools planned
    F. Tools actually used
    G. Contractors
    H. Safety requirements.

2. The system produces a report of all work orders which can be sorted by its current status in the work order flow (waiting on materials, waiting on contractors, ready to schedule, in progress, etc.).

3. The system tracks work order backlog:

    A. By craft
    B. By crew
    C. By department
    D. By planner
    E. By supervisor
    F. Any user-defined parameter.

4. The system allows work order retrieval from the equipment history to allow for historical job planning.

5. The system will flag any work order planned for equipment still under warranty.

6. The system updates the status of a work order:

   A. Manually
   B. Automatically.

7. The system uses the following priority system:

   A. Production assigned
   B. Maintenance assigned
   C. Multiplier, using both maintenance and production
   D. Increased by aging.

8. Work order numbers are:

   A. Manually assigned
   B. Automatically assigned.

9. When planning a work order, you can access stores, personnel, tools, contractors, etc., without leaving the work order.

10. The system will produce a work order schedule:

    A. Daily
    B. Weekly
    C. Monthly
    D. It does not produce a schedule.

11. When the system schedules maintenance work, it:

    A. Lists all work in the backlog
    B. Lists all work in the backlog by craft or crew
    C. Lists the work by priority
    D. Lists the work by date needed
    E. Compares the man power available by week and balances it against the work load
    F. Compares the man power available by day and bal-

ances it against the work load for each day of the week.

Total   ____

Computerized Maintenance Management Check Sheet
Rate for importance: 3 (very) to 0 (not wanted)
Inventory and Purchasing

---

1. The system generates a spares reorder report when the quantity on hand drops below the minimum required.

2. The system tracks the unit price information for the stock items using:

   A. Average
   B. FIFO
   C. LIFO
   D. Other.

3. The system maintains bin location for each stock item.

4. The system maintains on-hand quantity for each bin location.

5. The system has the ability to do multiple warehouses.

6. The system allows for easy transfer from warehouse to warehouse.

7. The inventory system is integrated with the vendor's own purchasing system.

8. When the reorder point is reached, a purchase requisition is generated:

   A. Automatically
   B. Manually
   C. Combination.

9. The system maintains a vendor file for the spare part to be ordered and the unit price.

10. The system stores _____ vendors per part.

    A. 1
    B. 3
    C. 5
    D. Unlimited.

11. When the part is received, the system notifies the planner which work orders can now be filled.

    A. Automatically
    B. By manually searching
    C. Difficult to determine.

12. The system produces performance reports for the purchasing section, including:

    A. Overdue P.O's
    B. Inactive parts
    C. Inventory valuation.

13. The system automatically tracks part cost to the work order on an itemized basis.

14. Stores catalogs can be printed by:

    A. Stock number
    B. Part description
    C. Range for either.

Totals   ____

Computerized Maintenance Management Check Sheet
Rate for importance: 3 (very) to 0 (not wanted)
Management Reporting

1. The system requires reports to be printed:

    A. Daily
    B. Weekly
    C. Monthly

  D. Yearly

  E. Any interval the user chooses.

2. The reports produced by the system are:

  A. Just lists of information

  B. Exception reports

  C. Summary reports.

3. The standard reports furnished by the system are:

  A. Predefined

  B. Created by user-specified selection criteria.

4. The system allows reports to be:

  A. Printed

  B. Displayed on screen

  C. Stored on disk

  D. Exported to another program.

5. The system can sort the equipment history using multiple user-specified criteria, to allow for specific analysis of information.

6. The system has a report writer in addition to standard system reports.

7. The report writer was designed to be used by:

  A. System managers

  B. Managers

  C. Maintenance personnel.

8. The system has a maintenance budget reporting module.

9. The system reports and forecasts equipment downtime.

10. The system tracks equipment downtime costs.

11. The system allows for searches on partial keys.

Totals   _____

Computerized Maintenance Management Check Sheet
Rate for importance: 3 (very) to 0 (not wanted)
Implementation

1. Vendor will perform the following:

   A. Full turn-key implementation
   B. Software implementation
   C. Hardware installation
   D. Data gathering
   E. Data loading
   F. System training
   G. User training.

2. The vendor has fully documented installation plans.

3. The vendor will provide at least 10 installation references.

4. The vendor has the following personnel on staff (not consultants they use):

   A. Software experts
   B. Maintenance experts
   C. Training experts.

5. The vendor's system:

   A. Needs no customization
   B. Requires some customization
   C. Requires extensive customization.

6. The software can be installed by in-house personnel.

   A. Yes
   B. No, but the vendor doesn't charge to do it
   C. No, and the vendor charges a flat rate to do it
   D. No, and the vendor charges an hourly rate to do it.

Total   _____

Computerized Maintenance Management Check Sheet
Rate for importance: 3 (very) to 0 (not wanted)
Maintenance Software Analysis

---

1. System is able to be operated by maintenance personnel.

2. System is:

   A. Menu driven
   B. Command driven
   C. May use both.

3. The system has the necessary modules to meet our needs (e.g.,PM's, equipment, work order, inventory, etc.).

4. The system is:

   A. Single user
   B. Semi-multiuser
   C. True multiuser.

5. The system is written in:

   A. COBOL
   B. "C"
   C. A relational database
   D. Basic
   E. Other.

6. All system modules are closely integrated (posting updates all relevant files or databases).

7. The system has the ability to archive files and retrieve the files for reports spanning long time periods.

8. The system has a security system that is:

   A. Password protected at a menu level
   B. Password protected at a screen level
   C. Password protected at a field level
   D. Security customized menus for each user.

9. The system requires the following hardware:

   A. An IBM PC
   B. An IBM PC-LAN
   C. DEC-VAX series
   D. AS-400 series
   E. Mainframe series
   F. Prime
   G. An IBM-compatible PC
   H. UNI-SYS
   I. Data General
   J. HP
   K. Is not hardware dependent.

10. How long has the product been on the market in its present form?

    A. 1 year
    B. 2 years
    C. 3 years
    D. 4 years
    E. Longer than 5 years.

11. When was the last major release of the software?

    A. Less than 1 year
    B. 1 to 2 years
    C. Over three years.

12. Does the system display analysis information in a graphic format?

    A. Yes
    B. No.

13. How is the on-line help available?

    A. Menu level
    B. Screen level
    C. Field level.

14. Are the fields edited for correct entry?

   A. All are edited
   B. Over half are edited
   C. Under half are edited
   D. None is edited.

15. Has the package been integrated with:

   A. Payroll
   B. Accounts payable
   C. General ledger
   D. MRP or MRP II
   E. In a CIM environment.

16. Are there lookup tables which can be displayed to select entries into the field, which the system will automatically insert into the field?

Total   ____

Computerized Maintenance Management Check Sheet
Rate for importance: 3 (very) to 0 (not wanted)
Vendor Issues

---

1. Vendor has the following:

   A. A user base of 20 or more sites (all referenceable)
   B. A plan for site visits of similar size and type operations
   C. Two or more years of experience in marketplace
   D. References and testimonials.

2. Vendor has on staff:

   A. Programming support
   B. Maintenance support
   C. End-user support
   D. Visionary support.

3. Vendor has:

   A. Documented product plans
   B. Programmers to maintain the system code
   C. User group.

4. Vendors personnel are compatible with my organization.

5. What is the financial standing of the vendor?

   A. Good
   B. Average
   C. Poor.

6. How many systems have been implemented (not sold) in the last 12 months?

   A. Less than 10
   B. 10–20
   C. 20–30
   D. 30–50
   E. Over 50.

7. Is there a user hotline and telephone support?

   A. 24 hours a day
   B. Normal business hours
   C. Not available.

8. How long is the software warranty?

   A. 30 days
   B. 90 days
   C. 6 months
   D. Greater than 1 year.

Total   _____

Computerized Maintenance Management Check Sheet Rate for importance: 3 (very) to 0 (not wanted) Summary Check Sheet	
1. Equipment Information	____
2. PM Section	____
3. Work Orders	____
4. Inventory and Purchasing	____
5. Management Reporting	____
6. Implementation	____
7. System Considerations	____
8. Vendor Considerations	____
Totals	____

Selection Tips

While all packages have their place in the marketplace, there are some points that need to be discussed.

Point #1. Be cautious when dealing with consulting firms selling "their" software.

This is important because many firms sell the software as a way of getting their consulting services into a facility. Be sure you are aware of what you are buying and the length of any support service and its price. Some firms will sell the software and charge for a support service that may run for many months. When they charge between $800 and $1500 per day for this service, the bills can mount up rapidly.

Point #2. Be cautious when dealing with firms that have developed their software for in-house use.

Generally, these firms will try to conform your organization to their software rather than the other way around. They are generally higher priced, since the companies are trying to recover their development costs. The support may be minimal and they may lack sufficient personnel to properly oversee and consult during the installation. Also, once the company has recouped their development costs for the system, they may not market it any longer. Be sure the company plans on staying in the computerized maintenance management system arena before purchasing the system.

Point #3. Do not hire someone just to computerize your present manual system.

Prepare the necessary paperwork so they understand what you are doing and your maintenance philosophy. If they try to computerize what you now have, it will not do much to increase your efficiency.

Point #4. Select a system that will grow with you.

If you start with a micro-version, be sure the manufacturer makes a mainframe version that you can upgrade to. Also, be sure your micro-purchase price can apply (at least partially) to the purchase price of the mainframe software.

Point #5. Do not develop your system in-house unless you do not need it for a long time.

Most in-house systems will take countless meetings and changes before it will be a reality. It is cheaper to select an off-the-shelf program that closely meets your needs. The only time this should be considered is when no program suits your needs; and this is highly unlikely given the present number of vendors.

Point #6. Do not select the hardware and then shop for your software.

This may restrict your choice of programs. It is best to select the software first, then buy the matching hardware.

Point #7. Price the entire package, not just the software.

Many companies add extra costs that do not show up until they are asked for. Be sure you understand what you are buying and how much service is included.

Point #8. Thoroughly check the reputation of the vendor you are dealing with.

There is no better method than to call sites where the system is presently in operation. This will help you understand the level of satisfaction the customer has with the product. To be fair to yourself and the vendor, try to check at least three different sites.

Point #9. Understand the difference between the vendor's maintenance agreement and licensing agreements.

Some vendors will sell you the package as-is, with the option of subscribing to a maintenance fee; this provides you with updates and software service support for the year. This is not a required feature. They will sell you the software and you do not have to have the ongoing support. There are firms that use a licensing agreement and require you to pay a yearly fee, i.e., there is no option. Be sure you understand the package you are buying, or there could be unanticipated costs.

System Justification

Management will be concerned about justifying the purchase of a computer system. Gathering some of the following cost records will assist in financial justification of the purchase.

Introduction

Maintenance is a function that, within most corporations, most people do not understand. Unfortunately, too many people think they understand the maintenance function. This is evident by the many differing methods currently used to organize and perform maintenance in American corporations. It is no secret that many corporate and plant executives have concentrated on operations or manufacturing management, while management of the more technical disciplines such as maintenance have been ignored or placed in a secondary status. Maintenance, for example, has been viewed as an necessary evil—an insurance policy, where money is paid and nothing (in their lifetime) is ever seen as a return.

In an effort to become more competitive, managers are turning over every stone to find areas for improvement and cost savings. As they study the maintenance function, companies have found that maintenance makes up anywhere from 15 to 40% of total product cost. They also are discovering that dollars saved in maintenance are a cost avoidance. If they take the typical profit margins for manufacturing companies, they discover that $1.00 saved in maintenance costs contributes as much to company profits as $3.00 in new sales. In larger companies, reducing maintenance expenditures by $1 million contributes as much to profits as increasing sales by $3 million. In the competitive markets that all companies find themselves, being able to improve maintenance and decrease unnecessary maintenance expenditures by $1 million is much easier and likely to occur than finding $3 million in new sales.

The following are guidelines for calculating possible savings which a company may achieve by implementing improved maintenance policies and practices with a Computerized Maintenance Management System (CMMS). The purpose of the material is to present a different examination of the effect of maintenance on a company's costs. The material is broken down to allow for various parts to be included or omitted as necessary. This will allow a company to customize the cost justification to meet its own circumstances.

Standard Cost Justification

This portion of the cost justification is composed of four main parts:

maintenance labor costs

maintenance material costs

project cost savings

downtime / availability costs.

Maintenance Labor Costs: Maintenance productivity in most American companies averages between 25 and 35%. This translates into less than 3 hours per 8–hour shift of hands-on activities. Most of the lost productivity can be attributed to:

waiting for parts

waiting for information, drawings, instructions, etc.

waiting for the equipment to be shut down

waiting for rental equipment to arrive

waiting for other crafts to finish their part of the job

running from emergency to emergency.

While 100% productivity is an unrealistic goal for any maintenance organization, 60% *is* achievable.

The productivity of maintenance technicians can be improved by concentrating on basic management techniques, such as:

planning jobs in advance

scheduling jobs and coordinating schedules with operations

arranging for the parts to be ready

coordinating the tools, rental equipment, etc.

reducing the emergency work below the 50% level by P.M.

With computer assistance, planning time per job is reduced, resulting in more jobs planned and coordinated. This results in more time for preventive maintenance activities, which in turn helps to reduce the amount of emergency and breakdown activities. This results in fewer schedule changes and helps to increase the productivity by reducing travel and waiting times. Successful users of CMMS have indicated an increase in productivity of 28%.

Maintenance Material Costs: The material costs are related to the frequency and size of the repairs made to the company's equipment. The sheer number of parts, in addition to the stores policies, purchasing policies, and overall inventory management practices, contributes to the overall maintenance material costs. Since little attention is paid to maintenance materials in some companies, inventories may be higher than necessary by some 20–30%. This increases inventory holding costs and makes materials unnecessarily expensive. The inability of the stores to service the maintenance department's needs results in "pirate" or "illegal" storage depots for just-in-case spares. This practice also drives up the cost of maintenance materials.

Good inventory controls enable companies to lower the value of the inventory and still maintain a service level of at least 95%. This enables the maintenance department to be responsive to the operations group, while increasing their own personal productiv ity. Successful CMMS users have averaged 19% lower material costs and an overall 18% reduction in total inventory.

Project Cost Savings: In many companies, maintenance is involved in project, outage, or refurbishing activities. These activities, if not properly controlled, can have a dramatic impact on a company's production capacity. The reason for this is that these activities are usually performed with the equipment in a down condition. This means there is no production during this time. For this reason, any time that can be eliminated from the project, outage, or refurbishing can be converted to production time.

Improved planning and coordination can be achieved with a CMMS. This will often help to shorten the downtime, even if the company is currently using a project management system. Successful CMMS users have indicated an average 5% reduction in outage time.

Downtime/Availability Costs: These costs are the true savings for a company determined to improve maintenance policies and practices. Downtime cost for equipment may vary from several hundreds of dollars per hour to literally hundreds of thousands of dollars per hour. One company has several production lines in its plant, with the downtime on each being worth $1 million for 24 hours.

In some companies, levels of downtime can run as high as 30% or more. This results in lost sales opportunities, unnecessary expenditures for capital equipment, and it generally puts the company in a weak competitive position. By dedicating the company to enforcing good maintenance policies and practices and utilizing the CMMS as a tracking tool, equipment downtime can be reduced dramatically. Successful CMMS users have averaged a 20% reduction in equipment downtime losses.

Maintenance Labor Costs

1. Time wasted by personnel looking for spare equipment parts (averages)

No inventory system	= 15–25%
Manual inventory system	= 10–20%

Work order system and inventory
   system   = 5–15%
Computerized inventory and manual work
   order system   = 0–5%

2. Time spent looking for information about a work order
   Manual work order   = 5–15%
   No work order system   = 10–20%

3. Time wasted by starting wrong priority work order
   Manual work order system   = 0–5%
   No work order system   = 5–10%

4. Time wasted by equipment not being ready to work on (still in production)
   Manual work order system   = 0–5%
   No work order system   = 10–15%

5. Total of all percentages of wasted time
   (1 + 2 + 3 + 4)

6. Total number of craftsmen

7. Multiply the figure obtained in 6 by 2080 (normal hours worked by an employee for a year)

8. Multiply the percentage totals by the total number of hours for all craftsmen (5 × 7)

9. Enter the average labor rate including benefits for a craftsman (sometimes called burden rate)

10. Multiply the potential savings (in hours) by the average labor rate (9 × 8)

11. Multiply the figure in line 10 by the percentage from the table below that best describes your facility:
   No work order or inventory system   = 75–100%
   Manual work order system   = 50–75%
   Manual work order and inventory
      system   = 30–50%
   Computerized inventory and manual
      work order system   = 25–40%

12. Total Savings: This will represent the projected savings from labor productivity.

Labor Explanation

The explanation for the labor cost justification is provided by the above form. On line 1, you would enter the total percentage of time the craftsmen are engaged in looking for materials. Each company will have varying averages depending on its current material control system and the level of reactive maintenance and advanced planning functions. It is not necessary to time study the maintenance technicians since a good estimate will suffice. The time wasted should include lost time at the start of a job, during the job, and returning the unused materials to the stores at the end of the job.

Line 2 is the time spent trying to determine exactly what work was requested on the work order. This is caused by insufficient work order descriptions such as: "It's broke, fix it" or "Repair or replace as necessary." The more vague the details are on the work order, the higher the percentage of time technicians will spend looking for additional details.

Line 3 is the time spent due to fluctuating priorities. If the technicians start one job in the morning and, after starting it, are pulled off to work on other jobs, there is a subsequent loss of productivity. The more often technicians are moved from job to job, the higher this percentage of wasted time will be.

Line 4 is the percentage of time wasted when the technicians go out to the job and the operations or production department has changed its schedule and will not release the equipment for maintenance. This type of delay occurs more frequently in plants where breakdowns cause production departments to frequently alter their schedules.

Line 5 is the total of all the waste percentages. If you have other types of productivity wastes, you should add this percentage of wasted productivity to the number on this line. Again, this can be as high as 50–80%.

Line 6 is the total number of craft technicians at the site that will be affected by (or are using) the CMMS for planning and scheduling.

Line 7 is the result of multiplying the number of technicians in line 6 by the average hours worked in a year by the technicians. This number will be 2080 hours for a straight 40–hour week for an entire year.

Line 8 is the result of multiplying the total number of hours worked by all technicians from line 7 by the total of all the wasted time percentages from line 5. This gives the total number of labor hours wasted in a year.

Line 9 is the average labor rate for the technicians.

Line 10 is the result of multiplying the average labor rate from line 9 and the total number of labor hours wasted in a year from line 8. This should show the potential savings in dollars for the labor.

Line 11 requires you to identify the present condition of your organization. Finding the correct range and then estimating your present level of control in the maintenance and stores area allows you to identify what part of the amount from line 10 that you will be likely to save.

Line 12 is the result of multiplying the percentage from line 11 by the potential savings in dollars from line 10. The result will be the total dollar savings the CMMS and the related maintenance controls should make in your labor productivity.

Inventory and Stores Savings

1. Total dollar value of maintenance spares purchased per year
2. Percentage of time that spares are already in stores when others are purchased

No inventory system	= 25–30%
Manual inventory system	= 10–20%
Computerized inventory system	= 5–15%

3. Savings total (cost avoidance)
4. Additional savings (inventory overhead)

    Multiply line 3 by 30%
5. Estimated total inventory valuation
6. Estimated inventory reduction

No inventory system	= 15–20%

Manual System (obsolete or unnecessary
    spares)   = 5–10%
7. Estimated one-time inventory reduction
    5 × 6
8. Estimated additional savings
    Multiply line 7 by 30%
    (Holding cost reduction)
9. Number of stockouts causing downtime
10. Amount of downtime (in hours)
11. Cost of downtime (per hour)
12. Total cost of materials-related downtime
    10 × 11
13. Percentage of savings obtainable
    Current controls poor   = 75%
    Current controls fair   = 50%
    Current controls good   = 25%
14. Savings in materials-related equipment downtime
    12 × 13
15. Total Savings
    3 + 4 + 7 + 8 + 14

Inventory and Stores Savings Explanation

The explanation of the stores savings begins with the total value of spare parts purchased each year. This number should be as accurate as possible and include all parts bought through plant purchasing, parts charged to blanket or open purchase orders, parts stocked or maintained by vendors, and parts ordered as direct buys.

Line 2 is the percentage of times the spare part could be found somewhere in the plant; however, since it was not easily found or it was not known at the time where it was located, it was purchased unnecessarily. The percentages indicated are ranges to be used depending on the current status of the organization.

Line 3 is the value of the spare parts from line 1 times the percentage indicated in line 2. This is a cost avoidance quantity and applies mainly during the first year of CMMS usage. After the first year, the stock quantities should be under more disciplined control.

Line 4 is the stock reduction from line 3 times the average holding cost for spare parts. In most companies, 30% is an acceptable estimated holding cost percentage. If your actual holding cost percentage is known, use it instead of the 30% estimate.

Line 5 is the total dollar valuation of the inventory currently on hand for the company. This should include the "private" or "pirate" stores held by various employees or crews. It should also include all major spares as well as normal items. Items put in long-term storage (grave yards or bone yards) should also be included.

Line 6 is the estimated reduction in total spares for the company. The percentages are based on the current mode of inventory control. The fewer the controls or the lesser the adherence to the inventory control disciplines, the higher the percentage of waste that potentially could be eliminated.

Line 7 is the result of multiplying line 5 by line 6. This will be the estimated dollar reduction for the inventory. This will be a one-time inventory write down. This is typically the largest savings a company will experience during the first year of the CMMS implementation.

Line 8 is the result of multiplying line 7 by the same holding cost percentage used in line 4. Again, in most plants, 30% is an acceptable value. If your actual holding cost percentage is known, you should use it.

Line 9 is the actual number of stockouts experienced by the stockroom that resulted in equipment downtime. This number should be less than the total number of stockouts. The less inventory control currently in use, the higher this number will be. In stockrooms with little or no control, the percentage of stockouts could be as high as 40% of all requests. The reverse of this is the service level. The service level would correspondingly be in the 60% range. The percentage of these stockouts resulting in downtime is also proportional to the amount of reactive maintenance performed by the company. If the company has little inventory control and is operating with reactive maintenance, then as much as 50% of all stockouts could result in equipment downtime. This translates into 20% of all stockroom transactions resulting in an equipment delay. The range from reactive organizations to proactive organizations would be from 20% to 1% of total transactions resulting in equipment downtime. If you have actual, reliable percentages, they should be used.

Line 10 is the total equipment downtime resulting from the stockouts. If this number is known, it should be used. If this number is not known, it may be derived by looking at all maintenance work orders resulting in equipment downtime and getting the percentage of all these work orders requiring materials. Using this number, in conjunction with the information from line 9, a close approximation of the total stockout-related equipment downtime could be obtained. If these figures are not available, industry averages run from a high of 40% to a low (for organizations with good inventory controls) of 2%.

Line 11 is the average cost of downtime for the company's equipment. If an average amount is not available, it may be feasible (if good records are available) to calculate the actual downtime for each piece of equipment and enter the total for all equipment in line 11.

Line 12 is the result of multiplying line 10 and line 11. This should result in the total material-related downtime for the plant.

Line 13 is the percentage of the downtime likely to be eliminated by improved inventory controls. This percentage will be based on the current level of inventory controls. The percentages shown are industry averages.

Line 14 is the result of multiplying line 12 by line 13. This should be the total equipment downtime costs that could be saved by implementing good inventory controls.

Line 15 is the total of lines 3, 4, 7, 8, and 13. This should be the total of all projected material savings for the company.

Major Project, Outage, and Overhaul Savings

1. Number of major outages and overhauls per year
2. Average length (in days) of outage or overhaul

3. Cost of equipment downtime in lost sales
   Use hourly downtime rate times total hours of
    outages
4. Total estimated cost per year
   $1 \times 2 \times 3$
5. Estimated savings percentage
   No computerized work order   = 5–10%
   Project management system   = 3–8%
   Project management system and inventory control
    system   = 2–5%
6. Total Cost Savings
   4×5

Project, Overhaul, and Outage Explanation

Line 1 is the total number of major projects, outages, and/or overhauls that are completed each year. For the project, outage, or overhaul to be used in this total, it must result in equipment downtime, production loss, or delays.

Line 2 is the total number of days for all of the major projects, outages, and/or overhauls for the company. Again, these must be days of downtime for the equipment resulting in production loss or delays.

Line 3 is the average cost of equipment downtime per day for the equipment impacted by the major projects, outages, and/or overhauls identified in lines 1 and 2. These costs are usually incurred when the equipment capacity is required, or when the resulting downtime requires the product to be diverted or delayed.

Line 4 is the result of multiplying line 2 and line 3. This is the total equipment downtime costs for all of the major projects, outages, and/or overhauls for the company.

Line 5 is the percentage of the total equipment downtime related to major projects, outages, and/or overhauls for the company that could be saved if good maintenance controls were implemented. The averages are based on the current controls presently utilized by the company.

Line 6 is the result of multiplying line 4 and line 5. This will produce the total projected saving from better controls on the company's major projects, outages, and/or overhauls.

Equipment Downtime Costs

1. Percentage of equipment downtime for year
   (If not known, use the estimate: average for industry is 5–25%)
2. Total number of production hours for equipment for year
3. Total of all lost production hours per year
   (1 × 2)
4. Multiply total lost production hours for year (from line 3) by your percentage from the table below:

No work order system	= 25%
Work order system	= 20%
Work order and stores inventory system	= 10

5. Total of downtime hours saved
6. Cost of downtime for 1 hour
7. Total downtime cost savings
   (5 × 6)

Optional Savings Considerations:

8. Total direct labor wages and benefits times the total of all lost production hours
9. Lost sales for year (divide the total sales for year by the total number of yearly production hours; multiple this figure by the total downtime hours saved)
10. Increased production costs to make up production lost due to downtime. (This would include the extra labor required on weekends or off-shifts to operate the equipment, extra energy costs to operate the equipment, etc.)

Downtime Costs Savings Explanation

Line 1 is the percentage of equipment downtime for the company. In order to obtain the total value for the plant equipment downtime, it may be necessary to calculate this section for the major critical pieces of equipment. The values given are industry averages. These should only be used if your actual downtime is not known.

Line 2 is the total number of production hours the equipment was scheduled for per year. Since the downtime is only accumulated when the equipment is scheduled to operate, this number must be derived from the production schedule.

Line 3 is the total number of lost production hours per year, obtained by multiplying line 1 and line 2.

Line 4 is the percentage of line 3 that could possibly be saved by implementing the disciplined controls in a CMMS. This percentage is based on the current condition of the company. The industry averages listed provide guidelines for the possible savings.

Line 5 is the result of multiplying the percentage in line 4 and the lost production hours in line 3. This is the total number of downtime hours that are projected to be saved by implementing the CMMS.

Line 6 is the cost of 1 hour of downtime for the production equipment used to compile the total in line 3. The number on this line may vary from equipment to equipment within the plant. You may take an average cost for all of the equipment, or perform the calculations in this section for each individual piece of equipment and total the individual sums.

Line 7 is the result of multiplying line 5 by line 6. This total is the downtime savings projected by implementing the controls and disciplines of a CMMS.

Line 8 is an optional consideration for downtime cost savings. It is the wages and benefits for the total number of idle operator hours incurred during the equipment downtime. This is typically calculated by multiplying the downtime hours by the number of operators assigned to the equipment. In some cases, this value is already added into the equipment downtime cost figure. If this is the case, this value should not be used.

Line 9 is another optional consideration for downtime cost

savings. It is the value of the lost sales for the plant. This value is only usable if the plant is in a sold-out condition and the downtime resulted in a lost sale for the product. The value would be the amount of the product not produced during the downtime.

Line 10 is another optional consideration for the downtime cost savings. It is the increased production costs to make up the product lost during the downtime. These costs are somewhat more difficult to determine, but would include the extra wages paid to the operating and maintenance staffs to cover the new production times scheduled; this is usually 1.5 times their base rate. These costs would also include the additional equipment utilities charges for operating the equipment when it should have been down. There are also other paperwork charges incurred for changing material flows, transferring materials from the equipment to storage and back to the equipment, etc.

The value of lines 8–10 should be added to the total in line 7 if they are applicable.

Total Projected Savings

1. Total maintenance labor costs savings
2. Total inventory and stores savings
3. Total project, outage, and overhaul savings
4. Total equipment downtime costs savings
5. Total savings possible from system installation
   (1 + 2 + 3 + 4)
6. Total projected price for system, including hardware, software, support agreements, training, and implementation costs
7. Payback
   (6 ÷ 5)

Detailed Cost Savings

The savings suggested in this section are somewhat more difficult to calculate for most companies, since they require some data to be known or accurately estimated. Where available, industry averages or ranges are given as guidelines for companies not possessing complete internal data.

Warranty Costs for Equipment

In many companies which have recently purchased equipment, this is an area of possible savings. In many instances, some of the maintenance repairs made on equipment under warranty are reimbursable under the purchase and service agreement with the equipment supplier. The amount of the reimbursement can vary, but companies have found that 5–10% of all work performed on equipment covered by warranties can be reimbursable.

There are some considerations a company might want to make when investigating this area of savings. There are conditions that may make compliance with warranty provisions difficult.

* To be covered by the warranty, do the repairs have to be made by or supervised by a representative of the supplier company?

* If the repairs are made by internal technicians, does it void the warranty?

* What level of documentation must be provided to the supplier in order to collect under the terms of the warranty?

If the above or similar provisions would impact the warranty, the company may want to consider whether it is worth the effort. For example, what if a critical piece of equipment would have to remain shut down while waiting for the supplier representative to arrive and make or oversee the repairs? The cost of the downtime would no doubt quickly exceed the moneys that could be regained from warranty claims.

There are opportunities to receive reimbursements for repairs made to equipment under warranty. However, a company would want to make a serious cost/benefit evaluation before these are actively pursued.

Energy Cost Savings

In order to effectively calculate any energy costs savings, it would be necessary for a company to know its energy usage. If this is not known, industry averages can be used for a quick estimate of the savings. Studies by the engineering institutes and international companies have shown that a company can cut energy consumption at a plant by 5–10%, depending on its current maintenance effort. Companies with good maintenance programs would see savings in the 5% range. Companies with little or no preventive maintenance inspections and services would realize savings in the 10% range. Some examples of energy savings for typical systems follow.

Mechanical Systems

Some of the energy savings in mechanical systems would be defined by the type of preventive maintenance performed on some of the basic mechanical components. For example, how accurately are couplings aligned? Misalignment by even 0.003" can lead to energy loss through the coupling. This loss is typically displayed as heat energy in the flex member of the coupling and the supporting shaft bearings. Even elastomer couplings will display energy loss.

A second type of mechanical loss is V-belt slippage. Improve tension results in slippage during loading on the belt. This loss is again shown as heat in the contact area between the belt and the sheave. Chain and gear misalignment will also lose energy in the transmission area and bearings. Poor maintenance practices and preventive maintenance will contribute a 5–10% energy loss for mechanical power transmission.

Electrical Systems

As with mechanical systems, the energy waste in electrical systems will be determined by the condition of the electrical systems and the level of maintenance service performed on the systems. Typical energy losses occur in loose connections, poor motor conditions, including contamination insulating the motor thereby increasing the temperature of the motor and subsequently its energy consumption.

Improper or insufficient maintenance on mechanical drives will also increase the amount of energy required by the motor to drive the system. This, along with many other losses, will contribute to excessive energy requirements by electrical systems. As with mechanical systems, expect a 5–10% energy loss due to poor electrical system maintenance.

Steam Systems

Steam-generation systems have long been recognized as having potential to produce substantial energy savings for most plants. Steam trap inspection programs, energy-efficient boilers, and leak-detection programs have been utilized in reducing steam system losses.

Depending on the amount of maintenance performed on the steam system, energy savings from 5% to as much as 15% have been reported by companies initiating good maintenance practices.

Fluid Power Systems

Fluid power systems include both hydraulic and pneumatic systems. Energy wastes in these systems are generally related to leaks. Leaks can be internal or external. External leaks are easier to find since air will make noise and oil leaves a pool of fluid. These leaks waste energy since the compressor or pump will have to run more frequently for the system to operate correctly. In addition, hydraulic systems will require cleaning up the leaks, which is another form of energy waste.

Internal leaks are more difficult to detect, particularly when the leaks are small. They are usually identified by sluggish performance and, in hydraulic systems, excessive component heat. Again, the pumps and compressors must run more frequently to compensate for the leaks. These, and other energy losses, will account for energy losses of 5–15% in fluid power systems.

As seen from these examples, a 5–10% energy reduction in the plant can easily be attained by a good preventive maintenance system.

Quality Cost Savings

Since the maintenance department is responsible for the equipment condition, quality costs are impacted by poor maintenance practices. For example, what percentage of all quality problems eventually are solved by a maintenance activity? Even if the activity is performed by the operator, the activity is one of maintaining the equipment condition. In some companies, 60% or more of the quality problems are equipment related. In order to calculate the possible cost savings, the value of the annual production for the plant should be calculated. Next, the current first-pass quality rate should be determined. The difference between this and 100% gives the current reject rate.

The next step would be to determine the reasons for the rejects. Usually, a top ten list will provide the majority of the rejects. After examining the list, determine which causes have a maintenance solution. This is the percentage amount that could possibly be reduced. An estimate of what percent of all the maintenance-related losses could be eliminated by a good maintenance program must be made. This percentage times the dollar value of the company's annual product will produce the possible quality-related savings. This number should then be added as a line item to all of the previous savings.

Paperwork/Clerical Savings

This section looks at the decrease in paperwork and clerical support that a CMMS requires compared to the manual method that most organizations are using. The current time required may be supplied by maintenance clerks, planners, supervisors, or even the maintenance manager. If the responsibilities are spread over multiple individuals, use the average labor cost for the calculation. Since this section is larger, a form will be utilized.

Maintenance Paperwork/Clerical Cost Justification Form (Use Weekly Averages)

1. Amount of time to plan work orders
2. Amount of time to post time to work orders
3. Amount of time preparing management reports
4. Amount of time to update equipment histories
5. Amount of time to generate weekly schedules
6. Amount of time spent preparing PM's
7. Amount of time spent preparing bill-of-materials for the weekly schedule
8. Time spent on other maintenance-related clerical activities
9. Total maintenance-related paperwork/clerical time per week (total lines 1–8)
10. Anticipated reduction in clerical/paperwork time required (usually 20%)
11. Total hourly savings (9 × 10)
12. Average hourly clerical/paperwork cost
13. Total dollar savings from clerical/paperwork improvements (11 × 12)

Clerical/Paperwork Savings for Stores/Inventory (Use Weekly Averages)

1. Amount of time to issue parts to work orders
2. Amount of time to post material charges to work orders
3. Amount of time preparing inventory reports
4. Amount of time to perform receiving functions
5. Amount of time to restock inventory items
6. Amount of time spent staging work order materials
7. Amount of time spent performing window issues for maintenance materials
8. Time spent on other inventory-related clerical activities
9. Total inventory-related paperwork/clerical time per week (total lines 1–8)

10. Anticipated reduction in clerical/paperwork time required (usually 20%)
11. Total hourly savings (9 × 10)
12. Average hourly clerical/paperwork cost
13. Total dollar savings from clerical/paperwork improvements (11 × 12)

Clerical/Paperwork Savings for Purchasing (Use Weekly Averages)

1. Amount of time to prepare purchase requisitions
2. Amount of time to consolidate purchase requisitions
3. Amount of time preparing purchase orders
4. Amount of time to update purchase order history
5. Amount of time to generate purchasing reports
6. Amount of time spent contacting vendors for pricing
7. Time spent on other purchasing-related clerical activities
8. Total purchasing-related paperwork/clerical time per week (total lines 1–7)
9. Anticipated reduction in clerical/paperwork time required (usually 20%)
10. Total hourly savings (8 × 9)
11. Average hourly clerical/paperwork cost
12. Total dollar savings from clerical/paperwork improvements (10 × 11)

Clerical/Paperwork Savings for Engineering (Use Weekly Averages)

1. Amount of time to find drawings for work orders
2. Amount of time to update equipment drawings
3. Amount of time updating PM program
4. Amount of time performing failure analysis
5. Amount of time performing reliability engineering
6. Amount of time spent providing information to the maintenance organization
7. Time spent on other maintenance-related engineering clerical activities
8. Total maintenance engineering-related paperwork/clerical time per week (total lines 1–7)

9. Anticipated reduction in clerical/paperwork time required (usually 20%)
10. Total hourly savings (8 × 9)
11. Average hourly clerical/paperwork cost
12. Total dollar savings from clerical/paperwork improvements (10 × 11)

New Capital Investment Savings

This section of the cost justification will require the budget for capital equipment replacement for the current year, or the projection for the next year. Once this is known, it is necessary to know the current type of maintenance activities. For example, is the company reactive or proactive in its maintenance practices? Is the company currently utilizing good preventive and predictive techniques? The formula for calculating this savings is as follows:

N.C.R. $ × A% = Projected Savings in New Capital Investment

N.C.R. $ = New Capital Replacement Dollars Budgeted

A% = The percent savings to be achieved. This is based on the current condition of the maintenance organization.
Currently reactive = 30%
Preventive = 20%
Preventive & Predictive = 10%

Additional Purchasing Savings

There are three main areas under consideration in this section. Whether these savings can be used by any company depends on if the described function currently exists. The three areas are:

buyer performance

volume pricing from vendors

blanket supplier contracts.

Buyer performance can be increased by as much as 25% if a company doesn't have a good maintenance planning and scheduling system in place. Calculating the savings for this area uses the formula:

# of Buyers × # of hours spent (each) on maintenance purchasing × Savings % = Total Hours Saved.

Multiplying the total hours saved by the hourly rate for the buyers will provide the total dollar savings for the increased buyer performance.

The volume pricing from the vendors is obtained by tracking the total volume of business awarded each vendor for the year and negotiating discount percentages on future purchases. This technique is only successful if the number of vendors is narrowed down to a select few, and if close track of all expenditures is kept. Depending on the level of business with the vendor, discounts of 3–10% are possible. This percentage would be calculated for the volume of business done with each vendor.

The effective use of blanket contracts can be utilized to have the vendor store many of the plant's spares and supplies in their warehouses, and only charge the company upon usage. There will be no holding costs, and the size of the inventory can be reduced. Many companies have successfully done this with fasteners, bearings, and other power transmission components. The supplier will also guarantee delivery within so many hours of the order. The company must, of course, guarantee the supplier a certain level of business each year.

Additional Inventory Savings

The additional inventory savings described in this section will be divided into three areas. The amount of savings in each area will depend on the current status of the organization and how much is currently spent in these areas. The areas are:

greater inventory turnover

reduced order expediting

better pricing from vendors.

Currently, the average for maintenance inventory turns in the U.S. is about 0.75 per year. "World Class" is considered to be 1 turn per year. Turning the inventory over more frequently allows for more capital to be free for investment. Calculating the savings in this area requires the total inventory valuation and knowing the number of turns per year currently. The difference between this number and the goal of 1 turn per year times the inventory valuation will identify the possible savings in this area.

The reduced order expediting savings will require knowing the amount of money spent on expediting spare parts for maintenance in the last year. The savings will depend on the current amount of reactive or short-term maintenance being performed. However, an average organization can expect a 50% reduction in expediting costs the first year.

The ability of the CMMS to track regular, blanket, and emergency purchases will help to identify the total dollar volume of business done with any single vendor. This will allow for negotiations with the vendor for a volume discount based on the total business done with the vendor. As mentioned in the purchasing section, discounts of 3–10% are customary.

Additional Accounts Payable Savings

The additional savings in the accounts payable area can be divided into the following three areas:

reduced invoice errors

more accurate and timely payments to vendors

increased accounting accuracy.

The reduced invoice errors come from having accurate information from ordering to purchasing to receiving to accounts payable. The computerized flow should reduce the invoice error level to below 2% of all invoices. Industry estimates show that it takes 1 hour of clerical time to correct an invoicing error. By comparing a company's present error level and estimating the savings if it is reduced, a possible dollar value can be derived.

The more accurate and timely payments to the vendors again results from having accurate information electronically available to all groups involved in the transaction. Reducing the errors and late payments can help the company avoid any overdue or unpaid charges from the vendors. The savings could be estimated by examining those charges for the last year and projecting a reduction of errors to the 1–3% level of all transactions. Examining the late charges in this light should show the resulting savings.

Increased accounting accuracy is based on the electronic accuracy of the information in the system. Additional billing and receiving errors should be eliminated, with the savings based on the current error level in the company. Again, a 1–3% error level is easily achievable.

System Implementation

This phase of purchasing a computerized maintenance management system can make or break the installation. If the implementation process is rushed or left incomplete, the system will not provide satisfactory performance. The implementation can be divided into the following steps:

1. updating all current records
2. system installation
3. data entry
4. introductions to the system
5. training the appropriate personnel.

Updating Current Records

This phase of the implementation can be performed before the system arrives. While it may seem to be a waste of time and resources, it is imperative for the information to be as factual and up to date as possible. Inputting old, inaccurate information will cause all information produced by the system to be inaccurate. In the initial stages, this type of problem would cast doubt on the reliability of the system. It is suggested that you receive from the selected vendor the format in which the information is required to be input into the system. This will ensure that the information is compiled correctly. Generally, if you are buying a software package, some adjustments will be required.

The following is a list of typical activities required to achieve a successful CMMS implementation. The activities should be performed in this same sequence. There are certain critical activities that must be performed before the CMMS can be utilized. The following implementation steps list:

* the task,

* a brief description of the task,

* duration of the task, and

* manpower required to perform the task.

These estimates are based on typical-sized sites, with basic maintenance practices and maintenance record keeping in place. Sites with well-established policies and practices in place may take less time. Sites starting from "ground zero" in any given area will require more resources in this area.

The scope of the implementation project also will determine the required resources. For corporate CMMS implementations, it is necessary to form a "Corporate Steering Committee for CMMS implementation" to ensure consistent usage of the system from site to site. In addition, there are some policies and practices that should be applied at each site to ensure data integrity once the CMMS is in full use.

1. Establish the Site Implementation Team

The site implementation team should consist of a representative from each of the departments affected by the CMMS implementation. At a minimum, this would include:

Maintenance

Information Systems

Operations/Production

Facilities

Stores/Inventory

Purchasing

Engineering

Plant Management.

The team members must be able to commit the time to carry out their assigned tasks in a timely manner. The team leader should be from the maintenance department. This team should be established by the Corporate Steering Committee with input from the various departments as to personnel for the team. The time required will be 1 day per site.

2. Establish Secondary Site Implementation Teams

These secondary site implementation teams are assigned certain ongoing responsibilities and must act independently of the Site Project Committee (but still report to the Committee for co-ordination of activities) in order to accomplish their objectives in a timely manner. The seven teams recommended at this time would be as follows.

a) Communication and Employee Awareness—The charge of this team is to keep all plant personnel informed as to the progress and purpose of the CMMS implementation.

b) Equipment and Asset Numbering—The charge of this team is to give all equipment and assets a specific identifier. This team should coordinate its efforts with the other sites and with the Information Systems Department to ensure data consistency and that the data format will work with the CMMS.

c) Storeroom Part Numbering and Data Specification—The charge of this team is to ensure that the numbering scheme is consistent with the CMMS corporate scheme, and to specify what data must be collected on each item to ensure consistency and that the data will work with the CMMS.

d) Equipment and Asset Format and Specification—The charge

of this team is to specify the required information for each equipment item and asset. This team also will coordinate its efforts with other sites to ensure consistency of data and that the format works with the CMMS.

e) Equipment and Asset Preventive Maintenance Program Review—The charge of this team is to evaluate the current preventive maintenance program and make recommendations for changes that would improve the effectiveness of the program and ensure that the program and its format would work with the CMMS.

f) CMMS Procedure Review—The charge of this team is to review all activities at the site that will eventually be performed through the CMMS. The team will develop written policies and procedures for each department related to the identified activities. Some typical examples would include:

How to initiate a work order

How to plan a work order

How to request materials

How to initiate a purchase order

How to receive materials

How to change time and materials, etc.

This team should be made up of a representative from each area affected by the CMMS implementation. The representative must have authority to make policy decisions for his or her respective departments. This committee may be made up of individuals from the Site Implementation Team.

g) Training Committee—This committee is responsible for defining the training requirements for each of the users. This committee should be comprised of a representative from each of the organizations involved in the use of the CMMS.

Each team member from the above teams should receive training on the CMMS system prior to the committee beginning any activity. The training requirements for each team member will run from a minimum of 2 days to a maximum of 5 days.

3. Resource Commitment by Task

The following information details the approximate resources that are required to accomplish the basic tasks for system implementation. The resources are approximated based on similarly sized sites. Some resources are defined by the number of equipment items, stores items, and general data required by the CMMS system. (The sample data included are for example purposes only.)

    A. Communications and employee awareness program.
        Time required: 1 person for 2 hours per week for the length of the implementation.
    B. Review and Definition of the CMMS-Related Procedures and Organizational Adjustments.
        Time required: 320 hours (usually 4 people for 80 hours).
    C. Development of the Written CMMS-Related Policies and Procedures to Support and Define the Organization Defined in Step B.
        Time required: 160 hours (usually 4 people for 40 hours).
    D. Development of the Nameplate *Data Formats*—Equipment and Stores.
        Time required: 80 hours (usually 2 people for 40 hours).
    E. Development of Accounting Information Formats—Cost Centers, Account Codes, etc.
        Time required: 40 hours (usually 1 person).
    F. Review of Equipment/Asset Numbers, Descriptions, and Locations.
        Time required: 200 hours (usually 1 person).
    G. Development and Review of Employee and Trades Data Formats.
        Time required: 40 hours (usually 1 person).
    H. Development and Review of the Preventive Maintenance Program.
        Time required: 12,480 hours (6 people for 1

year). 4492 equipment items × 3 PM's per item = 13,476 PM's.

I. Gathering of the Nameplate Data for Equipment and Assets.

Time required: for 4500 items, 4500 hours (should utilize 2–4 people).

J. Gathering of All of the Nameplate Data for Inventory Items.

Time required: for 15,000 items, 15,000 hours (should utilize 2–4 people).

K. Development and Review of All Purchasing-Related Data Formats.

Time required: 120 hours (usually 3 people for 40 hours).

L. Assigning Spare Parts to Equipment.

Time required: 960 hours (usually 2 people for 3 months).

M. Purchasing Data Gathering.

Time required: unknown.

These estimated times can vary depending on the amount of data currently developed by the site. However, the data integrity must be completely accurate and valid. Any flawed data entered on system startup will guarantee flawed data later during system use.

This estimate does not include the time and resources required to enter the data once identified and gathered. If the data are gathered in the correct format, the entry time can be reduced by utilizing temporary data entry clerks. It is not recommended that plant personnel be utilized to enter the data into the CMMS system.

Summary:

Project A	14 months × 8 hours	112 hours
Project B	4 people × 80 hours	320 hours
Project C	4 people × 40 hours	160 hours
Project D	2 people × 40 hours	80 hours
Project E	1 person × 40 hours	40 hours

Project F	1 person × 200 hours	200 hours
Project G	1 person × 40 hours	40 hours
Project H	6 people × 2080 hours	12,480 hours
Project I	4 people for 1125 hours	4,500 hours
Project J	8 people for 1875 hours	15,000 hours
Project K	3 people for 40 hours	120 hours
Project L	Unknown	
Total Hours Required		33,052 hours

Using this number (total hours required) as an approximation means that it would require about 16 people dedicated for a 12-month implementation period. It appears that in order to implement the CMMS, it would required a 12–14-month implementation period. If the resources are constrained, the implementation could easily go over the 16–24-month time period. Implementations over 16 months have a greater failure rate than those in the 12–14-month time period.

This model *assumes* that there are currently good maintenance organizational controls in place, with an auditing system for the maintenance function, and a proper level of maintenance supervisors and planners.

With the implementation of CMMS taking this long, the other plants will likely become frustrated as they "wait their turn." It might therefore be advisable to do parallel implementations, with a large and a small site. One large site could start the process; one of the small sites, which would require fewer resources, could be started within a short time period afterwards. This time period should be 1 month or less. Once the smaller site is up and running, then the next smallest site could be started. When the larger site is finished, the next larger site could be started.

Proposed CMMS Implementation Flow Process

1. Establish the Corporate Steering Committee for CMMS.
2. Establish the site implementation team.
3. Establish site project teams.
4. Promote a "kick-off" meeting for site and project teams.

5. Install hardware and the CMMS software.
6. Initialize the CMMS software.
7. Provide initial training for the site and project teams.
8. Define organizational procedures for CMMS use.
9. Develop the written CMMS-related procedures.
10. Restructure the organization—if required.
11. Begin the development of various data collection formats.
12. Use the formats (defined in step 11) to begin the data collection process:
    a. equipment
    b. stores
    c. PM's
    d. personnel
    e. purchasing
    f. accounting.
13. Begin the data entry process using the same order as in step 12.
14. Begin end user training on the CMMS system.
15. Establish stores stock levels—physical count.
16. Begin use of work order system.
17. Monitor all usage of the CMMS system closely for the first week. Gradually loosen monitoring for the next 30 days.
18. Audit the CMMS system usage at the end of 30 days for problems.
19. Continue 30-day audits for the first 6 months of system use.

Installing the Software

This process may need to be done in two different steps. If the system is just the software, it will be a matter of loading the programs into the system and making sure that they work properly. If the entire system—hardware and software—is purchased, the installation becomes a little more complicated. The hardware will need to be installed in a clean location. The larger the system, the more room required for the hardware. Mainframes and some minicomputers need to be installed in a climate-controlled filtered area to prevent erratic operation of the system.

Some vendors will provide the necessary support to install the system. It would be advisable to have some in-house personnel working with the vendor, so that they have a better understanding of system operation.

Data Entry

This step takes all of the information in the current record keeping system and enters it into the computer database. This information will provide the basis for all decision making and reporting functions. If the present system is not up to date, the computerized system won't be either.

The way that the information is entered will also be important. All similar components should be labeled the same, for ease of cataloging data. The more uniform the information, the easier the system will be to use.

Do not underestimate the time it will take to enter all of these files. Large organizations will accumulate a tremendous amount of information over several years. This information cannot be entered into the system in one day by one employee.

For sites with limited resources, it has been found that hiring temporary help will be the most economical method for inputting the data.

System Introductions

This step is important to the system's success. If the system is not presented to the users in a positive manner, the effectiveness can be reduced. It is important for the groups to accept the computerized maintenance management system as a tool for them to use. If it is introduced as "big brother," to watch that they do their jobs better, the employees and supervisors may be reluctant to use the system.

If employees and front line supervisors do not cooperate with the system, they can virtually negate any positive effects the system would have. If they are convinced that the system will help them do their jobs more efficiently, they can be great contributors to the success of the system.

It is more effective if the user groups are brought into contact with the system in smaller groups. If they can individually see the action of the system, they will gain confidence in the system and its purposes.

System Training

As with any tool, it will only be effective if it is used correctly. Training will ensure that the various groups will be able to use the system. This is often the most overlooked part of the program. The vendor should offer a good training program. Use the training time built into the system price (or if it is an additional cost) to train several key individuals on the operation of the system. Then use these individuals to help train the other users in the plant. If the vendor offers user and training manuals, be sure to obtain a sufficient supply of both.

It is not recommended that you buy a software package and attempt to get by without training. Even standard database or spreadsheet programs offer advanced training. Just look at the computer courses at vocational schools or community colleges: if programs at that level require training, imagine how much more training will be needed for programs that are as advanced and complicated as CMMS. If the training is not taken, you probably will never achieve the maximum benefit from the system. Also, if the vendor does not offer training and support, you will have to question the quality of the system and support.

System Problems

The following are solutions to problems that have been encountered during the selection and implementation of computerized maintenance management systems. By becoming aware of the problems experienced by other installations, a manager can prevent their occurrence in the installation at his or her facility.

1. Do not try to accomplish unrealistic goals and installation times. Set reasonable goals for the manpower and time available.
2. Do not create extra permanent positions. This only contributes to the overall expense of the system.
3. Provide appropriate personnel during the data entry into the system. This will prevent personnel from taking shortcuts, while entering information, trying to meet deadlines.
4. Provide personnel to work with the vendor during installation of the system (both hardware and software). The knowledge gained may help prevent system problems in the future.
5. Provide adequate training for all personnel using the system. Untrained personnel will not use the system effectively, thereby contributing to less than optimal performance of the system.
6. Provide all computer workstations with a copy of the user manual and training material. No employee has a perfect memory; these materials will provide reference when problems develop.

Is it possible to do it right the first time when selecting and implementing a computerized maintenance management system? Many people, including industry experts, say no. But why is this the case? To understand why companies think they can't do it right the first time, you need to understand the common reasons for selection and implementation failures. A clear understanding of the problems makes the solutions obvious. The reasons for most failures, during the selection and implementation of maintenance management systems, can be divided into ten areas.

Problem #1. Failure to Assess Current and Future Needs

Most companies have 3- to 5-year strategic plans. These plans include details for manufacturing, product development, equipment procurement, workforce sizing, etc. After close examination, the question is "How many 3- to 5-year plans include maintenance requirements?" yet maintenance is a support organization. It needs to be included in such plans, or at least be privy to the contents of such plans. This will allow the maintenance organization to be proactive in making the changes required to provide the necessary support to other parts of the company. Still, most maintenance organizations are reactive, and this attitude is fostered by the mindset of upper management.

Rather than being able to focus on long-term goals, maintenance departments are focusing on short-term reactive situations. This contributes to many "false starts" or "taking the wrong path" as regards maintenance policies or programs. It is analogous to a marathon runner. You do not find many successful runners staring at their feet. Good runners are observant, constantly watching their environment, their competitors, looking for anything that might give them an advantage in the race. Maintenance departments must have a similar mindset. They must understand their current situation, but never lose sight of the goal of total competitiveness. This goal begins with providing:

the highest level of maintenance service

at the lowest possible total cost

and in a timely manner.

In far too many instances, the maintenance managers are either forced to or willingly watch their feet by focusing on short-term goals such as:

starting a preventive maintenance program

adding a maintenance technician

purchasing a CMMS

getting a vibration analyzer

and so on . . .

In doing these things, there is no long-range view of how to integrate these projects into a common, focused plan. So the manager will develop a disjointed organization, pulling in many different directions, without understanding how all the programs are only pieces of the whole picture. In considering the importance of the CMMS, revisit the Maintenance Management Maturity grid. Note the line for Maintenance Information and Improvement Actions; this line indicates the progress toward maturity for the maintenance information systems.

In many cases, maintenance managers will purchase a CMMS to generate preventive maintenance inspections, or generate work orders, or track inventory. But, as they achieve this goal, they want to make progress in other areas. In other words, their needs begin to change. Their current CMMS no longer meets these needs. Is it the fault of the CMMS vendor or the software? Clearly, the answer is NO! The vendor and software met the previously identified needs and provided the services they were required to supply.

The true problem is that the maintenance organization was never able to look beyond its current problems to plan for future needs or requirements. This will be damaging to the maintenance manager's career and also to the company's competitive position. When companies provide maintenance managers the information and ability to plan for the long term, this problem will be eliminated.

Problem #2. Failure to Properly Document the System Requirements or "Get User Input"

This failure is closely related to the first in that the requirements for the system must be identified before they can be documented. However, as noted on the grid, the closer the organization moves toward maturity, the more groups there are that use the information in the maintenance system. Consider the following questions.

Does the system provide stores and purchasing with its information?

Does the system provide accounting with its information?

Does the system provide engineering with its information?

Does the system provide upper management with the information they require?

If the maintenance information system does not provide the data for all the groups in a format and manner that is acceptable, then those groups will not use the system. If all groups cannot use the system, the true savings from having maintenance integrated into other parts of the company may not be realized. The organization will be forced into the "sneaker-net" mode of operation, which is neither responsive nor cost effective.

Beyond this part of the problem lies another in the same category—the lack of user input or consideration into the decision. For example,

Who can initiate a work order?

How many steps does it take?

Can the technicians look up related information?

How many keystrokes does it take to plan a work order?

So when a system is selected, it should have not only the functionality required to meet the user's needs, but should also have the ease of use necessary to make it acceptable to the users.

The third, and possibly most insidious, part of this problem is: who selects the maintenance software? In some cases, it has been

the inventory and stores department

the purchasing department

the MIS department

the engineering department

the quality control department

the accounting department.

While each of these groups should provide input into the decision, they should not and must not control the decision. The maintenance department must use the system to manage its organization and job responsibilities. If another group selects the software, it will not meet the needs of the maintenance organization. This leads to confusion and lack of competitiveness for the maintenance department. The cost for maintenance to do business will increase, the quality of maintenance work will decrease, and the timeliness of the completion of the work will suffer.

Consider for a moment the following questions.

> In how many corporations does the maintenance organization tell the MIS group what computers they can purchase for the company?

> In how many corporations does the maintenance organization tell the accounting department what software system to buy for accounting?

> In how many corporations does the maintenance organization tell engineering how to design or purchase corporate equipment?

> In how many corporations does the maintenance organization tell the purchasing departments what policies and practices to enforce and observe?

To select the right maintenance system, it must be driven by the maintenance organization that is going to use the software. While the support groups previously mentioned should have input into the decisions, they should never make the final decision. To allow this to happen is to ensure problems during the system implementation and operation.

Problem #3. Lack of Management Support

There are several contributing factors to lack of management support. The area of management support is very critical to the success of the program since a maintenance system crosses many organizational boundaries. Without the management support necessary to enforce certain disciplines that the system requires, the quality of the data produced by the system will be suspect. If the data are questioned, then each decision made based on those data also will be questioned. This contributes to the "why do this" attitude and quickly results in "suboptimization" or failure of the CMMS. For example, if the inventory and purchasing group will not use the maintenance system, or at least interface to it, the true effectiveness of the implementation will be 50% or less. The reason for this is that such a large portion of the maintenance costs are stores/purchasing related.

To obtain and keep management support, the benefits of implementing and using a maintenance system must be understood. This involves using key information from the first two problem areas (discussed previously), such as needs assessment and user participation. However, one more thing must be done to ensure management support: translate the benefits into dollars. This is the language spoken at the level where management support should be obtained. Without financial justification, the support necessary to make some parts of the organization work with the maintenance system will never be gained.

In addition to the initial support, there is the issue of ongoing support. This is especially critical in the time of economic downturns, since maintenance is one of the first areas in which some companies will make reductions. Companies making temporary cuts during these times sacrifice long-term benefits for relatively short-term gains.

The ongoing support is maintained by periodic benchmark reports. If the long-range plan was developed (see problem 1), such reports will establish where you are currently compared to where you said you would be. If you are ahead of schedule, document this point. If you are behind schedule, give the reasons why, and document what has been done to solve the problem.

The main point is to communicate—this is simply good business practice. This highlights the need for maintenance to be managed like a business, like all other parts of the company. This alone will notably contribute to maintaining management support.

Problem #4. Failure to Conduct a Good Search of the CMMS Marketplace

The CMMS marketplace is large and diversified. With over 200 vendors presently competing in the market, it can be a time-consuming and costly process to examine each of the packages. How can the process be simplified or at least reduced in complexity?

The first step is to take the requirements that were specified (in problem 2) and compile them into a reference document. This document should highlight the needs of the company as they relate to CMMS. This document can then be used to explain to the vendors your requirements for CMMS software. Depending on the complexity of the company's needs, the document can be as simple as a checklist or as complex as a request for a proposal. The more complex the requirements are, the fewer vendors that will respond to the document.

Identifying vendors can be as simple as picking up a directory of software vendors, such as the one provided in this book. But how can the number of vendors be reduced? If the computer hardware is predefined by corporate edict, this can be a limiting factor. If the hardware is Data General, Hewlett Packard, or Prime, the vendors that have software operating on these systems are few in number. If the hardware is IBM micro or compatible, then the vendor choice is more extensive.

A second method of narrowing the vendor list is to examine their participation in advertising, conferences, or seminars. Usually, only successful vendors participate in these activities. This also will help to narrow the list.

A third method is to consult with companies with similar processes or manufacturing techniques. By finding out which system they use, or which systems they considered during their selection process, your list of potential vendors can be shortened.

A fourth method is to use a consultant. Consultants can be useful, but they can also be a problem. Some key considerations when using consultants are:

Do they sell a package themselves?

Do they have an "arrangement" with one of the vendors?

Have they selected packages for one or many companies?

Obtaining answers to these questions will help you select a quality consultant for your project.

The bottom line of this problem is to be thorough in examining the market, but don't take too long. You will have a window of opportunity within your company to conduct a successful project. Don't let the window close before you get started.

Problem #5. Developing an In-House System

While this problem is not as widespread as it once was, it still occurs occasionally. The reasons for this problem usually fall into one of three categories:

1. someone did an incomplete search of the marketplace
2. someone feels that this would be easy to do
3. MIS or a programmer needs job security.

The point here is this: of the over 200 packages on the market, one should meet the needs of your organization. Developing in-house is an expensive proposition. You still must go through the needs assessment, but then you have programming time, maintenance's time, all the time for the related groups to examine and test, as well as support and modification time. In some cases, in-house development costs 10 times more than purchasing a packaged system.

Then comes the issue of ongoing support. The vendors have support personnel, as well as software enhancement programs. A company that does in-house development must staff these positions. What will this cost be? In some companies, this alone has added up to several millions of dollars per year. When this cost is added to the development cost, it quickly shows that in-house development is not a viable option.

The important point is that no matter how good in-house development looks, it is never as cost-effective or as permanent a solution as purchasing a packaged system.

Problem #6. Failure to Assess the Vendor's Qualifications

Once the selection process has begun, the vendor, its software, services, and consultants must be evaluated. In a market as large as the CMMS market, there are vendors of all sizes and qualifications. The challenge to each user is to find the vendor with the software and specific skills required to successfully complete their project.

Vendors may be required to provide some of the following services:

maintenance consulting

software consulting

hardware consulting

training

good documentation.

While the software is being specified, it also would be wise to define which services are going to be required from the vendor. Then, during the selection process, the vendor's capabilities to provide such services could be evaluated. It is also important to find out if the vendor has these resources as part of its organization or does it contract these services out to consultants. If it is a third-party service, it can develop into a logistical problem. It is always good business practice to check with previous clients, who have used these services, to find out their level of satisfaction.

Problem #7. Failure to Test the Software

This problem is related to the previous one. Just as you check out the vendor and its services, the software should also be checked for the desired functionality. All too often, companies will purchase the software based on what they saw during a demonstration. Then, once they have the software, they find it does not do everything exactly as they thought it should.

The best way to avoid this problem is to test the software for a specific time; usually, a week or two is sufficient. However, to be fair to the vendor, it is best to have one of their trainers on site during the testing. This ensures that you are using the software correctly and not overlooking any of the functionality. Expect to pay for the trainer's time while he or she is on site. This, again, is only fair to the vendor.

Also related to this problem is ensuring that the right people test the software. It does not do much good for a manager to test the software if he or she is not going to use it every day. It is best to use the planners, supervisors, stores clerks, etc. These end users will quickly let you know how the software works and whether or not it helps them to do their jobs.

This issue becomes even more important when you are purchasing customized software. The failure to check the customized package against the specified requirements has led to many problems for both the users and the vendors. This testing will avoid a potential problem as the system is implemented.

Problem #8. Failure to Plan the Implementation

Implementing a maintenance system takes resources. These resources may be financial, if you are having the vendor or a consultant do it. Otherwise, the resources will be in the labor required from your staff to implement the system. Implementing the system takes time; it does not happen overnight. During the implementation, it takes labor to gather data, and to input data into the computer. Failing to realize this, some managers have promised quick implementations and paybacks. When these were not delivered, the managers were dismissed or transferred.

Most of the vendors who have been in the marketplace for any time at all have documented implementation plans. You should ask for copies of the implementation plans for review. By reviewing the implementation plan, you will see how long the implementation should take for an organization of similar size and manufacturing process. This will enable the project to be set on a correct implementation time frame and budget.

Problem #9. Failure to Obtain Sufficient Training and/or Documentation

Many companies will still purchase software and try to "learn by the manual." It is a very costly and time-consuming method to learn the functionality of software. It is best to have the vendor's training personnel train your people. To allow the users to flounder, or even to let the vendor's *programmers* train your people, will spell sure disaster.

It takes a certain type of person to train for software use, and part of the selection process should include the evaluation of the vendor's training personnel. Again, it is a matter of reviewing the training program and personnel with existing clients. This will ensure that the program has produced satisfactory results.

The training and documentation process also suffers when companies try to reduce the cost of the system implementation.

One of the first areas they cut corners in is the amount of training or the number of sets of documentation. This will result in poor utilization of the system. Consider this question for a moment: "What are some of the most popular adult education programs?" Some course titles may include:

"Effective Use of D-Base"

"Mastering Symphony"

"Easy Uses for Lotus 1–2–3."

The point is that since people are willing to spend time and money to master $400–$500 programs, why would a company spend $10,000 or more and not train on the software? A company should not really expect to optimize the use of the software without training.

Problem #10. Failure to Estimate the Time Necessary to Collect and Load Data

This problem is related to problem 8. However, it is important enough to warrant a separate discussion. Just ask yourself: "How long does it take to gather and load the equipment, PM, and inventory information into a CMMS?" The typical project will require 1 hour per record. So if you have 10,000 equipment, inventory, and PM records, it will take about 10,000 hours to load the data. This will hold true whether the vendor loads the data or you load the data yourself.

Failure to properly estimate the time or cost to load the data has caused many projects to fail. Just be sure that you are aware of what the total cost and time will be for your project.

While companies will encounter other problems occasionally, eliminating the above ten will boost the total satisfaction rate for the marketplace. If you can eliminate these problems, you can *Do It Right the First Time.*

Long-Range Problems

Data–information–facts: whatever you call it, it is important to any manager trying to make good decisions. Producing good, useful data is the goal of any Computerized Maintenance Management System. Even as a CMMS is implemented, data collection begins. Consider the various modules used in a comprehensive system:

equipment

inventory

purchasing

personnel

preventive maintenance

work order

reporting.

The basic relationship of these modules is common to most systems. The equipment module requires a company to identify each piece of equipment or facility location that costing and historical repair information will be tracked against. The financial information stored in the equipment history is the basis for making repair/replace and other costly equipment decisions. The accuracy of this information is determined by the data provided by the other modules.

The inventory module requires a company to identify the spare parts carried in each stores location. The data required include (but are by no means limited to):

part number

part description (short and extended)

on-hand, reserved, on-order, max-min, etc.

locations

part costing information

historical usage.

The data provided by the inventory module are critical to accumulating accurate material costing information for each piece of equipment or facility location.

The purchasing module is included as part of the inventory module. The purpose of this module is to provide the planner with a window into the ordering information. Some of the information includes:

part number

part description

part costing information

delivery information (including the date)

related vendor information

the ability to order nonstock materials.

The importance of this module becomes clear when trying to plan a job without knowing when the part will be delivered and trying to estimate the job cost without knowing the new part cost.

The personnel module allows a company to track specific information about each employee. Some of the data required include:

employee number

employee name and personal information

pay rate

job skills

training history

safety history.

The data in the personnel module are required to ensure that accurate labor costs are posted to the work order and ultimately to the equipment history.

The preventive maintenance module allows the company to track all PM-specific costs. The costing information is drawn from the personnel and inventory databases. Some important information stored in the PM module include:

type of PM (lubrication, calibration, testing, etc.) and frequency required

estimated labor costs (from the personnel module)

estimated parts costs (from the inventory module)

detailed task description.

The collection of these data ensures accurate service information and costing each time the PM task is performed. The CMMS can also project labor and material resource requirements for calendar-based preventive maintenance tasks.

The work order module allows for different types of work orders to be initiated and tracked to completion, with the costing and repair information being charged to the correct piece of equipment or facility location. The use of the work order requires information from all other modules of the CMMS. Some of the information required on a work order include:

> identifying the equipment or facility location where the work is being performed
>
> identifying the labor requirements (personnel)
>
> identifying the parts requirements (inventory)
>
> the priority of the work
>
> the date the work is needed by (not ASAP)
>
> contractor information
>
> detailed instructions.

As shown, the work order requires information from all of the CMMS modules to be truly effective. Without the accurate information, the work order cannot collect the required data. Without accurate and complete data, the work order cannot post accurate information to the equipment history. Without accurate data in the equipment history, the maintenance manager cannot make timely and cost-effective decisions.

The reporting module ties together all the data gathered by all the modules into a meaningful form for analysis. Reports should provide analysis of the data collected, not just lists. Analysis reports should be short and concise, not lengthy and difficult to interpret. The types of reports generated by the CMMS determine the ultimate usefulness of the system to the company.

The importance, to the corporation, of data collection and analysis is highlighted by the following:

to *manage*, you must have *control*

to have *control*, you must have *measurement*

to have *measurement*, you must have *reporting*

to have *reporting*, you must collect *data*.

The timeliness and accuracy of the data collected by a CMMS, and their use by the company, spells success or failure of the system.

Once a company has purchased a CMMS, how long is it before accurate and informative reports can be produced? The answer depends on how long it takes the company to develop accurate data. In a recent survey conducted by *Engineer's Digest* and the AIPE, the majority of the respondents (over 70%) said that it took them over 6 months before the CMMS was fully operational. Taking the survey data one step further, over 40% took over 1 year to make the system fully operational. The information collected by these companies will have some value before the system is completely implemented, but the data will not be completely accurate until the system is fully utilized. For example, if only certain departments are on the CMMS (a typical pilot implementation problem), then the data from these departments may be accurate; but in areas where there is a crossover or combination with another area or craft, the data may be incomplete or distorted.

As highlighted previously, a CMMS is designed to provide a completely integrated data collection system. However, even with mature users, many are not getting complete (and thus accurate) data from their CMMS. In the *Engineer's Digest*/AIPE survey, mentioned above, respondents were asked about their usage of the inventory, purchasing, and personnel modules of their systems. One question showed that the majority of the respondents are using less than 70% of their system. A second question broke this into modules with the following results:

inventory—52% use the CMMS inventory

purchasing—32% use the CMMS purchasing

personnel—35% use the CMMS personnel.

Since the CMMS modules are not being used for these functions, what *is* being used? Some companies are using other corporate systems; but over 25% of the respondents are not using any method to collect this information. Even when other corporate systems are being used, are the data accurately being posted in the equipment history? In the majority of the cases, the posted data are not accurate (or not even posted), and so the equipment history is incomplete or inaccurate.

To illustrate this, consider your local garage. When you take your car in for repairs, the service manager gives you an estimate of the time and cost of the job (work order planning). You accept the estimate and the work is scheduled and started. When the job is completed, you are given a shop order with a complete breakdown of each part used and its related cost. The bill (work order) also shows the number of hours the mechanic worked and the hourly rate. The total is then the sum of the labor and parts. You expect this bill each time you go to the garage for any work. If you were given a bill with only the final price, i.e., with no breakdown, you would not accept it! Does your CMMS reporting give you accurate costing breakdowns for your equipment?

For example, when using a CMMS, if the inventory information is not closely integrated, the planner cannot be assured of the accuracy of the stores information if it is only updated once per day or once per week. This situation arises many times when other corporate systems are "interfaced" to a CMMS. Hours could be wasted looking for a part that is supposed to be in the stores, when in fact the part was used the previous day or shift. While this delay seems inconsequential, when downtime costs range between $1000 and $100,000 per hour, these types of delays may mean the difference between profit and loss for the entire company.

When it becomes time to consider replacing your car, do you look only at the labor charges you have made against it for its life? Do you look only at the parts you used? NO! You consider the whole picture—labor, materials, its present condition, etc. It is ridiculous to think that these principles do not carry over into the asset management programs at our companies! Yet companies have set the CMMS information flow so that the material costs or labor costs are not shown on the work order or equipment history. Any decisions they make will be based on inaccurate or incomplete data, and will be mistaken. The financial implications of these decisions could spell disaster for a company by placing it in a condition where it cannot compete with a company making full use of a CMMS and obtaining the subsequent cost benefits.

The Solution

The solution to the problems encountered with CMMS installations where the data are not being properly collected is to re-evaluate the current use of the system. What data are being collected accurately? What data are incomplete or missing? What parts of the CMMS are we not using correctly or not at all?

By evaluating the answers to these questions and then working to provide accurate data collection, the CMMS usage can be beneficial to the bottom line. In the competitive marketplace that every company currently finds itself, it is unacceptable to make guesses when data can be provided. The cost benefits obtained by making correct decisions will help to make a company more competitive. Wrong decisions could put a company out of business by taking it out of a competitive position.

What reports should a company utilize within a CMMS? There are some systems available with no reports, while others have hundreds of "canned" reports. The deciding factor regarding the use of reports is to utilize the reports you need to manage your maintenance function. If the report does not support or verify an indicator that you utilize to manage maintenance, it is not beneficial but burdensome. Reports that produce hundreds of pages of "data" that are never used are worse than useless—they can overload the already busy maintenance manager. If you measure maintenance by the estimated versus actual budget, and the CMMS cannot produce a budget report, then it is not supporting your organization. With CMMS reports, too many are just as bad as too few.

Since management requires measurement, and measurement requires data, each company must fully utilize its CMMS to obtain these data. Remember:

> without data, it is only someone's opinion;
>
> discussions require factual data; and
>
> arguments occur when emotions and opinions are involved.

At your company, do you have discussions or arguments? The answer to that question may mean the difference between being a "World Class" competitor and being a second-rate company.

Conclusion

Following the guidelines provided in this section will assist management in justifying and selecting a computerized maintenance management system. Selection of the system should be a well-researched and logical decision. Purchasing a system that provides the needs—and not the wants—will assist in making the selection cost effective. By not purchasing an expensive system that is beyond the requirements of the installation, the computerized maintenance management system costs can be easier to justify.

Implementation should also be a smooth and logical procedure. Proper preparation and training will contribute to an effective installation.

Computerized maintenance management systems will become standard at all progressive installations in the future. Management will have to decide if it is time for their facility to invest in this useful tool.

The Future

Where will the future in this field lead us? What are the trends in the systems? Should I buy now or later?

We will briefly consider some observations regarding these questions.

The future seems to be moving in the direction of the automated factory. Maintenance will be a key ingredient here. System vendors are already providing interfaces to the system for equipment monitoring. As the equipment needs it, it requests its own maintenance based on given engineering parameters set at installation.

The future trend in the systems seems to be integration of all modules in the systems. It should eventually be possible to interface the systems with almost any computer system in the factory. The multiuser PC versions of the systems seem to be the next goal of most vendors. This allows the user to enter information from various workstations into one central PC. The advances in hardware always allow the opportunity for advances in the systems. Only time will tell what will occur here.

The buy-now-or-later question is always asked. It is a waste of money not to implement a system and begin the savings immediately. The system can be upgraded or changed as new enhancements are made. It is important to select a capable and qualified vendor who is willing to support his or her product from the beginning.

During the development of any maintenance tools, there are growth and development cycles. For example, consider the development of vibration analysis equipment. At first, these devices were very complex, difficult to use, and required extensive training to be proficient. As the products matured, the equipment became easier to use, the data became easier to understand, and the systems made predictive maintenance programs easier to manage.

Just as the predictive maintenance systems have improved and advanced, the computerized maintenance management systems (CMMS) have also shown the same trend. Recently, several major vendors in the marketplace have introduced new products or features to their present product lines that indicate the next generation of maintenance software is now arriving. We will explore these new advances in the following areas:

1. functionality
2. languages.

Functionality

The definition of the term functionality, as applied to maintenance management systems, is the activity controlled or monitored by the software. As any beginner shopping for their first maintenance software package can attest to, most of the packages have standardized on the same functionality. They all seem to have the same basic components, including:

1. work orders
2. preventive maintenance
3. equipment information
4. inventory
5. purchasing
6. reports.

If you were to talk to 20 or 30 vendors, and request their literature, reading it would produce an overlapping matrix of information. The varying sized systems would all sound alike, yet show a big difference in price, thus leading the prospective buyer to ask "What is the difference?" The difference is how the software accomplishes the task. For example, ask the following questions.

How many keystrokes does it take to enter a work order?

How many reference or "cheat" sheets does the user have to refer to in order to perform a function?

How much manual manipulation of the data is required to achieve the desired results?

These types of questions will begin to show the differences. So while most of the main functions are standardized within the systems, the steps the users have to take vary dramatically.

Some options being included in the "new generation" packages include the following.

1. Maintenance scheduling. Some systems merely produce

lists of work orders in the craft backlog; others have so-phisticated scheduling algorithms allowing the computer to do what it does best: analyze and sort data. The "new generation" maintenance software packages are providing user-defined scheduling parameters to produce schedules set to the priorities established at each of the client sites. This allows for maximum flexibility and utilization of the maintenance workforce. They have the flexibility to sched-ule by craft, crew, department, or other parameters, mak-ing the schedule more useful in MRP, MRP II, JIT, or CIM environments.

2. The ability to produce "analysis" reports. In the past, most reports were unintelligent lists. In the new systems, reports are meaningful, producing information such as exception reports, statistical analysis, and optimization reports.

3. Predictive maintenance enhancements is another area where the vendors are working with existing predictive maintenance systems to provide transfer of information. This allows some trigger in the predictive maintenance sys-tem to produce a work order in the computerized mainte-nance management system to correct a potential problem. Several vendors have working versions of this type of sys-tem in operation.

4. Interfaces versus integration. This is a lesson in semantics. Most vendors will say they can "integrate" their package with almost any other existing software package. But is that what they really mean? An interface is the passing of data between two systems. The data are generally then acted on in a "batch" mode. Integration is a "real time" transfer of data between two systems. Each system will re-spond immediately to the data instead of waiting for a cer-tain process to be run. It is easier and quicker to integrate the data with "new generation" software than some of the older systems.

Prospective buyers must keep one point in mind: almost all CMM vendors interface; very few have working models of integration. In addition, integration is much more expensive than interfacing. You should be sure of your needs before asking for integration.

Language

The latest "buzzwords" from the system side include "4th GL," "Relational Database," and "User Interfaces." What do these terms mean to the prospective buyer of maintenance software?

The 4th generation languages (GL) are new computer languages which are superior to the older 3rd generation languages in many areas. For example, it can be as much as ten times faster to develop a software system in a 4th GL than in a 3rd GL. This allows the vendor to produce a package, maintain it, and add new features much more quickly than in the past. This is an important advantage because the vendor will be able to utilize new technologies in a more timely fashion. Experts also agree that the 4th GL's have the following advantages:

1. programs are easier for the vendor to maintain
2. programs are easier for the vendor to debug (important for customized systems)
3. the programs are more user friendly
4. they give programs "platform independence."

Some try to refute these advantages by saying that 4th GL's operate more slowly and that the application (i.e., CMM software) will not run as quickly as it would if it was written in a 3rd generation language (such as COBOL, FORTRAN, & PASCAL). Most experts agree that such statements fail to acknowledge that 3rd GL's require far more programming code than 4th GL's to accomplish the same function. When this is considered, the speed contest between the 3rd and 4th generation languages becomes a virtual toss-up. To help ensure satisfaction, a serious buyer should request that the vendors benchmark their system's performance and guarantee a predefined level of performance.

"User interfaces" is another common buzzword. It basically means the tools a user has to work with within the system. User interfaces include: pop-up windows, point-and-shoot selections, touch screens, and graphics. When examining these features, we find they have several advantages. Pop-up windows allow the vendor to program data windows to appear when the user is inputting data into key fields. The windows will usually contain the allowed entries for the field. This removes the necessity for the users to have an open manual at their terminals or to have a "cheat-sheet" taped to their workstations. The pop-up windows may also be used to bring up help screens, other program information, or messages from other users.

"Point-and-shoot"-type selections are often used on pop-up windows or on information inquiry screens. Point-and-shoot selections allow the user to move the highlighted bar up or down the screen; when the desired selection is highlighted, the user presses another key to insert the selection into the desired field. No retyping of the selection is required. This ensures that the data are accurate, and reduces the amount of typing required by the user. The "point-and-shoot" selections and "pop-up windows" are trademarks of software written in 4th generation languages.

Touch screen technologies have existed for some time, but have just recently been applied to maintenance management software. Touch screens allow the user to answer a question, choose from a menu, or highlight a graphic display, merely by touching a predefined section of the computer screen. Because this is more of a hardware function than a software function, most systems can use this technology. However, there is a difference between being able to use the technology and having written a software package to take advantage of the technology. Using it to operate a standard menu-driven system is different than using it with a system adapted for touch screen technology. For example, one system allows the user to look at a graphical display of the plant, press a general geographical area, and have the area displayed in more detail. From this detailed diagram (usually an equipment layout), the user can press the symbol for the piece of equipment desired. The system will then allow the user to write a work order, look at equipment parts, or examine the equipment history. One system even lists a selection of typical problems for the piece of equipment, and when the user selects one, fills out a work order automatically. The ease-of-use rating for that system would have to be very high.

The down side of touch screen technologies for a maintenance or general plant environment is that you have to have clean hands, otherwise, you spend the time you gain using touch screens cleaning the screen so you can see what you are doing. How useful and how much acceptance this technology receives, only time will tell.

Graphic displays of maintenance analysis information is also a mark of the "next generation" of maintenance software. The days of looking a columns of figures have given way to days of enhanced graphs displaying trends or total information pictures. For example, it's much easier to look at a graph of the maintenance backlog for the last 6 months than it is to look through the totals column. Graphs and charts make much more effective management presentations and reports than do pages of lists. Graphic displays of maintenance data will be gaining popularity and will soon be a requirement of most CMM systems.

"Platform independence" is another buzzword gaining popularity. Platform independence means the software package runs in a basically unaltered state on most hardware platforms. This allows the CMM program to be developed on almost any computer system and directly posted to another without programming modifications. Therefore, a vendor may have a package running on a standalone PC, a local area network, and a minicomputer, all written in the same language with the same operation. The advantage to this is that if you are buying for several sites, one could use a microcomputer (PC), one could use a local area network (LAN), and one could use a minicomputer. All three would produce the same reports, have the same system flow, and require the same basic application training. If a site starts to outgrow its system, you can move it up to the next level of hardware and regain the performance, without losing continuity or requiring extensive retraining. This is also quite an advantage to companies who want to start small and grow a system.

Platform independence is a feature of most 4th generation languages. In fact, one source recently stated that ORACLE (a common 4th GL) can run on 55 different hardware platforms.

S.Q.L. (structured query language) is another term now becoming a buzzword. S.Q.L. is becoming an emerging industry standard for data structure. This makes it easier to extract and report with data from various systems. One CIM integrator said that S.Q.L. could become the means by which the various parts of the factories of the future would communicate. S.Q.L. compatibility would then become an important factor in picking a computerized maintenance management package. In a recent listing of 4th generation languages, over 60% boasted of S.Q.L. compatibility with many others announcing plans to become S.Q.L. compatible in the near future. This trend could be an important one to watch for where integration with other packages for automated information flow is a consideration.

The Future

What maintenance management software will be available in the future that we don't have today? The following are often overheard in discussions of some Research and Development staffs:

artificial intelligence or expert systems,

enhancements for different organizational environments,

more sophisticated and enhanced hardware and software combinations.

Artificial intelligence or expert systems have many different meanings, depending on who you are speaking to; however, to CMM users, they will be guides to equipment troubleshooting and repair. For example, if a problem developed on an equipment component, the repairman could go to a menu for the type of equipment. By selecting the symptoms the equipment is displaying, the solution to the problem could be derived. Of course, the obvious problem is having the necessary background to construct the troubleshooting information. It will be interesting to watch this feature develop.

Enhancements for various environments will be developed, such as systems for companies with Total Productive Maintenance, MRP, MRP II, Computer Integrated Manufacturing, and Just-In-Time plants. These will be written to enable the users to optimize their performance in each environment. The information and user interfaces for these systems will be a challenge to develop. Again, these areas will be interesting to watch develop.

Development in hardware and software operating systems and languages is another area where changes are frequently occurring. The development from the IBM-PC, to the XT, to the AT, and to the new PS group occurred over a relatively short time period. However, look at the amount of power now available for an economical price. Tasks that used to take large mainframe computers considerable time to accomplish can now be quickly solved by small mini- or microcomputers at a fraction of the cost. The future holds the 486 chips, new processors, new computers, and new software languages. How the CMM vendors will apply this technology is the third area that deserves attention in the future.

Conclusion

As past maintenance markets have grown and matured, it now seems that the computerized maintenance management systems market is taking steps to achieve that goal. With the demands that the factories of the future, world market competition, TPM, MRP, MRP II, and JIT environments are putting on maintenance organizations, the maturing is essential.

The question becomes—as the vendors work to increase the quality of the software to meet "world class" standards—are we doing the same for our maintenance organizations and the people that make them up?

Computerized Maintenance Management Trends

A current overview of the direction of computerized maintenance management software provides some interesting insights into the current status of maintenance management. Currently, the software trends are focusing on the following areas:

1. support for TPM
2. support for predictive systems
3. utilization of expert systems
4. interfaces with CAD and imaging systems
5. integration with production scheduling systems (MRP/MRP II).

Support for TPM

One of the current trends in maintenance management is the shift towards TPM (Total Productive Maintenance). This concept ties together the various parts of an organization around the utilization of the equipment. The benchmark to this concept is the overall equipment effectiveness formula. The formula requires the delay times for the equipment, the capacity utilization rate, and the quality rate. While most vendors offering this option are doing so on a manual entry basis, when afforded the opportunity, the CMMS interfaces with the production scheduling control system to provide the input electronically. This feature is enhanced by allowing access to the CMMS data by all involved personnel. This requires the vendors to ensure that their software has "easy to use" features so that all personnel can utilize the system for data entry and analysis.

Support for Predictive Systems

While some vendors have offered the ability to pass data from predictive systems to the CMMS, the interfaces are becoming more sophisticated. Some of the latest interfaces allow for automatic Preventive Maintenance service order generation based on the current reading from the predictive system, with some allowing for repair work order generation automatically, if the condition becomes too severe. In addition to predictive interfaces, several vendors have developed "real time" interfaces for their systems to allow input from PLC's (Programmable Logic Controllers) to trigger a maintenance request, similar to what the predictive systems will generate.

Utilization of Expert Systems

Several vendors are currently offering the ability to set troubleshooting guides or tables within their software, allowing the user this "rough" form of an expert system as a start. Future enhancements to their systems will include tying this system to the equipment histories to allow for probabilities of failures and performing statistical analysis. Other vendors are working with troubleshooting and expert system vendors to develop interfaces, allowing for the power of these tools to be accessible to the maintenance and engineering organizations.

Interfaces with CAD and Imaging Systems

Some vendors have offered interfaces with Computer-Aided Design systems (such as Autocad) for several years; however, the level of sophistication and ease of use of these features are increasing. The newer interfaces are allowing for linking the drawings to the equipment records, thus permitting the users quicker, easier access to the drawing information. The use of imaging system interfaces allows the users to store not only drawings, but also part information and details, vendor's equipment manuals, and other technical information on the computer system. The user can then access the information from any appropriate terminal in the plant, eliminating the need to go to a technical library to retrieve information. The ability to access this information will help expedite repair and replacement.

Integration with Production Scheduling (MRP/MRP II)

This is a sophisticated interface, since a company must have excellent MRP/MRP II scheduling practices in place as well as accurate (at least 95%) schedule compliance for the maintenance organization. Since there are only a few (approximately 10%) companies in the U.S. that are successful with MRP/MRP II implementation, and even fewer companies with high-level maintenance organizations, this interface is virtually nonexistent. It has been discussed by consultants, but is highly oversold since there are so few companies that achieve this level of proficiency with both the production and maintenance organizations. Only the future will determine the value of this type of interface to the manufacturing and process environments.

ISO-9000 and Maintenance

The ISO-9000 is a set of suggested standards which businesses are being asked to comply with by the European marketplace. These standards are identified as:

ISO-9000—organizations and nomenclature

ISO-9001—design/development, production, installation, and servicing

ISO-9002—production and installation

ISO-9003—final inspection and test

ISO-9004—quality system guidelines.

This standard, when complied with, provides assurance to all customers that the company's product meets high quality standards. How do the standards involve maintenance? It is clearly shown you cannot produce quality products on poorly maintained equipment. When work bearings or high wear areas exceed normal tolerances, then products will be hard to keep within specification. But we don't need ISO-9000 to teach us this. However, the side of ISO-9000 that some people will overlook is the record keeping and documentation to prove the production process is in control. For example, the 9004 standard covers the calibration and certification of all measuring and test equipment involved in producing the product. The standard highlights the need to identify the instruments, recalibration schedule, recall procedures, calibration instructions, installation, and use. In addition, when instruments are found to be outside acceptable limits, the cause for the deviation must be determined, and a solution to prevent any recurrence must be implemented.

The process or production equipment is also covered in the 9004 standard. One part of the standard states that a program of preventive maintenance should be established to ensure continuing process capability. In his book *ISO-9000*, Brian Rothery, a European ISO-9000 registrar, said: "As far as ISO-9000 is concerned, it is a fundamental fact that one cannot operate a factory to satisfactory quality management level without a preventive maintenance program." Yet many companies are rushing to the ISO-9000 registrars with new documentation in hand, but without a defined process to continue to produce the new data. The basic maintenance tracking systems, whether manual or computerized, are an absolute necessity if a company is to be ISO-9000 certified. While a company may put the documents together the first time, what about the future? One major difference between ISO-9000 and the Malcom Baldridge Award is you don't "win" ISO-9000 certification, you achieve it. Unlike the Malcom Baldridge award, you can lose ISO-9000 certification. An ISO-9000 company must be recertified periodically, as part of an ongoing program.

A third area which may impact maintenance is the training requirements. Each operator and maintenance technician is to receive training to understand the ISO-9000 standards. In addition, employees are to be trained in the proper operation and care of the instruments, tools, and machinery used in the performance of their job assignments. In some areas, the company is required to certify the employees.

With the current recession, companies have been cutting back in all departments, including maintenance and training. Each company is now faced with the issue of having the proper staff to collect and maintain the equipment and instrumentation at the proper level, and to record the necessary data to be ISO-9000 certified. Will corporate and plant management step up to the issue or will they pay "lip service" to ISO-9000? Only time will answer this question.

Computerized
Maintenance
Management
System Vendors

Computerized Maintenance Management System Vendors

ABC Technologies Inc.
1700 El Camino Road
Suite 409
San Mateo, CA 94402
(415) 377–0492

Adatek, Inc.
700 Airport Way
Sandpoint, ID 83864
(208) 263–1471

Anawan Computer Systems
19 Winterberry Lane
Rehoboth, MA 02768
(508) 252–4537

Application Systems
Corporation
400 MacArthur Blvd.,
Suite 2030
Newport Beach, CA 92660
(714) 757–7070

Anderson Consulting
901 Main Street
Dallas, TX 75265
(214) 741–8735

Austin Consulting
Austin Company
9801 W. Higgins Road
Rosemont, IL 60018
(312) 696–0500

Auto Tell Services
600 Clark Avenue
King of Prussia, PA 19406
(215) 768-0200

Avila Associates, Inc.
3505 Cadilac Ave. Building D
Costa Mesa, CA 92626
(714) 754-0994

Bender Engineering
3535 Farquhar Ave., Suite 2
Los Alamitos, CA 90720
(213) 598-4741
(Recommended: Small PC)

Bonner & Moore
2727 Allen Parkway
Houston, TX 77019
(713) 522-6800
(Recommended: Mainframe)

Business Solutions
601 Ridge Avenue
Evanston, IL 60202
(312) 866-7728

CK Systems
772 Airport Blvd.
Ann Arbor, MI 48108
(313) 665-1780
(Recommended: Small PC)

Cadworks
222 Third Street, Suite 1320
Cambridge, MA 02142
(800) 866-4223

Candlewood Computer
Services
4 Oakwood Drive
New Fairfield, CT 06810
(203) 746-1181

Centaurus Software, Inc.
4425 Cass Street, Suite A-1
San Diego, CA 92109
(619) 270-4552

Cerberonics, Inc.
The Koger Center,
Number 18
Suite 220
Norfolk, VA 23502
(804) 455-5282

CHAMPS Software, Inc.
1255 North Vantage Point
Drive
Crystal River, FL 32629
(904) 795-2362
(Recommended: AS 400,
DEC Mini, IBM Mainframe)

Clayton Systems Associates
7907 Jaguar Trail
St. Louis, MO 63143
(314) 644-7122
(Recommended: All PC's)

Cobro Corporation
4260 Shoreline Drive
St. Louis, MO 63045
(314) 291-8676

Comac Systems, Corp.
3 Speen Street
Point West Office Center,
Suite 310
Framingham, MA 01701
(508) 875-5991
(Recommended: Larger PC's)

Combustion Engineering
1515 Broad Street
Bloomfield, NJ 07003
(201) 893-6111

Cord Associates
2423 Allen Street-West
Allentown, PA 18104
(215) 433-5020

Creative Management
400 Riverside Ave.
Jacksonville, FL 32202
(800) 874-5554
(Recommended: Small PC)

Custom Computer Software
1108 Woodshire Drive
Knoxville, TN 37922
(615) 966-6832

DFM Software Systems
1601 48th Street
West Des Moines, IA 50265
(800) 922-4336
(Recommended: All PC's)

DP Solutions
207-MS Westgate Drive
Greensboro, NC 27407
(919) 854-7700
(Recommended: Small PC's)

DPC, Inc.
1015 Maurice Field Drive
Paris, TN 38242
(901) 642-8627

DSA Systems
105 Summerfield Park
Mashpee, MA 02649
(508) 477-2540

Data Group
77 S. Bedford Street
Burlington, MA 01803
(800) 247-1300

Datastream Systems
113 Mills Ave.
Greenville, SC 29605
(803) 235-8356
(Recommended: Small PC's)

Decision Dynamics
696 McVey Ave.
Lake Oswego, OR 97034
(503) 636-4310

Decision Systems
P.O. Box 432
1089 3rd Ave. SW
Carmel, IN 46302
(317) 846-1833

Diagonal Data
(HSB Reliability Services)
2000 E. Edgewood Drive
Lakeland, FL 33806-2242
(813) 666-2330
(Recommended: All PC's,
Also UNIX)

Dynacorp, Inc.
P.O. Box 18129
Rochester, NY 14618
(716) 265-4040

E-MAX
2420 Frankfort Ave.
Louisville, KY 40206
(800) 666-9400

EFFAX
444 N. York Road
Elmhurst, IL 60126
(312) 279-9292

El International
10050 N. 25th Ave.
Suite 306
Phoenix, AZ 85021
(602) 943-8962

EPC International
4000 MacArthur Blvd.
Suite 4400
Newport Beach, CA 92660
(714) 995-9031

Eagle Technology
5150 N. Port Washington
Road
Suite 2
Milwaukee, WI 53217
(800) 523-9131
(Recommended: Small PC's)

Electron Instruments
P.O.Box 745
Loveland, CO 80539-0745
(800) 833-1881

Elke Corporation
P.O. Box 41915
Plymouth, MN 554411
(612) 559-9394
(IBM AS-400?)

Emerson Consultants
207 E. 30th Street
New York, NY 10016
(212) 481-0330

Engineering Management
Consultants
7670 Woodway, Suite 230
Houston, TX 77063
(713) 789-0754

Epix, Inc.
1851 Sherbrooke St. E
Suite 100
Montreal, P.Q.
Canada H2K 4L5
(514) 522-3749

Ertl Associates
P.O. Box 590131
Houston, TX 77259
(713) 996–8430

Facilitech Systems
32500 Telegraph
Suite 205
Birmingham, MI 48010
(313) 645–1400

FBO Systems
950 E. Paces Ferry Road
Suite 3180
Atlanta, GA 30326
(404) 239–9539
(Recommended: Larger PC's,
Mini's)

Fleming Systems Corp.
1118 Roland Street
Thunder Bay, Ont.
Canada P7B 5M4
(807) 623–2310
(Recommended: DEC Minis)

Fluor Daniel
P.O. Box 19019
Greenville, SC 29602–9019
(803) 298–2752
(Recommended: DEC Minis)

Ambrose Frederic, LTD
10 Lisa Street
Bramela, Ont.
Canada L6T 4N4
(416) 453–2794

GBS Associates
240 Kent Road
Warminster, PA 18974
(215) 674–3949

General Energy Technologies
250 E. 17th Street
Costa Mesa, CA 92627
(714) 645–7733

Generation Systems
640 NW Gilman Blvd.
Suite 100
Issaquah, WA 98027
(206) 391–9046
(Recommended: All PC's)

GP Solutions
1776 22nd Street
West Des Moines, IA 50265
(800) 477–4968
(Recommended: All PC's,
UNIX)

Hansen Software
1745 Marchant Road
Sacramento, CA 95825
(916) 921–0883

Herbaty and Associates
253 Plainview Drive
Bolingbrook, IL 60440
(708) 759–1915

HSB Reliability Services
P.O. Box 2242
Lakeland, FL 33806
(813) 666–2330
(Recommended: All PC's,
UNIX)

Indus Group
60 Spear Street, 9th Floor
San Francisco, CA 94105
(415) 904–5000
(Recommended: Custom MF,
DB2)

Inova Systems, Inc.
11666 Wayzata Blvd.
Minnetonka, MN 55343
(612) 542–8910

International Development &
Research
5107 Leesburg Pike,
Suite 2603
Falls Church, VA 22041–3234
(703) 845–8155

JB Systems
21800 Oxnard St., Suite 1000
Woodland Hills, CA 91367
(800) 282–5277
(Recommended: Small PC's)

J&H Software
2000 W. Central Ave.
Toledo, OH 43606–3996
(419) 473–9611

Josali, Inc.
P.O. Box 460
Enka, NC 28728
(704) 252–9146

Kellogg Plant Services
P.O. 4557
Houston, TX 77210
(713) 753–3591

Kurtz & Steel USA
2500 City West Blvd.,
Suite 300
Houston, TX 77042
(713) 266–5604

Life Cycle Engineering
P.O. Box 300001
Charleston, SC 29417
(803) 556–7110

Lodestar Systems
1420 N. Clermont Blvd.
Claremont, CA 91711
(714) 625–0017

Logical Data
5240 Babcock St. NE
Suite 300
Palm Bay, FL 32905–4643
(406) 723–7000

Lohara Software Systems
5703 Cochran Ave.
Sun Valley, CA 93063
(805) 522–5793

Lucas Management Systems
12701 Fair Lakes Circle,
Suite 350
Fairfax, VA 22033
(703) 222-1111

M2 Limited
9210 Wightman Road,
Suite 300
Gaithersburg, MD 20879
(301) 977-4281

Macola, Inc
333 Center Street
Marion, OH 43302-4148
(800) 468-0834

Maintenance Automation
Corporation
3107 W. Hallandale Beach
Road
Hallandale, FL 33009-5121
(305) 962-8800
(Recommended: Small PC's)

Management On-Line
5301 Hollister, Suite 110
Houston, TX 77040
(713) 690-0697

Management Planning
Systems
P.O. Box 1968
Eugene, OR 97440
(503) 484-1004

Marcam Corporation
3365 Harvester Road
Burlington, Ont.
Canada L7N 3N2
(416) 632-6015
(Recommended: AS-400)

MFG Systems Corporation
100 Davidson Avenue
Somerset, NJ 08873
(908) 560-0010

Minneapolis Software
2499 Rice Street
Roseville, MN 55113
(612) 484-5684

Modern Management
7301 Carmel Executive Park
Charlotte, NC 28266
(704) 542-6546

MTI/McComas Technologies,
Inc.
3305 Dixie Highway
Erlanger, KY 41018
(800) 437-6785

Nanosoft
7575 San Felipe, Suite 325
Houston, TX 77063-1714
(713) 266-6266

Nielsen-PM Associates, Inc.
54 Church Street
P.O. Box 310
LeRoy, NY 14482
(716) 768–2282

OmniCorp
P.O. Box 332
State College, PA 16804
(800) 726–4181

Owen Engineering &
Management
5353 W. Dartmouth Ave.
Denver, CO 80227
(303) 969–9393

Panda Software
1907 Bardstown Road
Louisville, KY 40205
(800) 537–1694

PBM System One
P.O. Box 173
Sandy, OR 97055
(503) 668–3150

Pearl Computer Systems, Inc.
P.O. Box 1026
Mt. Laurel, NJ 08054
(609) 983–9265

Penguin Computer
Consultants
P.O. Box 20485
San Jose, CA 95160
(408) 997–7703
(Recommended: Very small
PC's)

Peregrine Systems, OOPS
1638 Pinehurst Ct.
Pittsburgh, PA 15237
(800) 852–8075
(Recommended: Small PC's)

Performance Associates
379 Diablo Road, Suite 212
Danville, CA 94526
(510) 838–7464

Phoenix Data Systems
24292 Telegraph Road
Southfield, MI 48034
(313) 358–3366

PMS Systems
2800 28th Street, Suite 109
Santa Monica, CA 90405
(310) 450–1452

Precision Maintenance
Systems
112 E. Clifton Ave.
Clifton, NY 07011
(201) 340–3458

Prism Computer Corporation
575 Anton Blvd. 3rd Floor
Costa Mesa, CA 92626
(714) 432–6476

Process Analyzer Resources
P.O. Box 106, Rte. 2
New Florence, PA 15944
(412) 676–9998

Project Services International
Robinson Plaza III, Suite 300
Pittsburgh, PA 15205
(412) 747–0111

Prototype Inc.
300 Drakes Landing,
Suite 270
Greenbrae, CA 94904
(415) 925–8000

PSDI
20 University Road
Cambridge, MA 02138
(617) 661–1444
(Recommended: Larger PC's)

QBIC
7529 Standish Place, Suite 113
Rockville, MD 20855
(301) 265–2690

Quest Software Systems
P.O. Box 57983
Murray, UT 84157
(801) 265–2024

Rainbow Enterprises
15127 NE 24th Street,
Suite 152
Redmond, WA 98052
(206) 881–7243

Rantac
P.O. Box 5663
Bellevue, WA 98006
(206) 451–1899

Raymond & Associates
5005 Newport Drive,
Suite 508
Rolling Meadows, IL 60008
(708) 577–6868

Remasco, Inc.
10240 SW 96th Terrace
Miami, FL 33176
(305) 271–9806

Revere Technology
One Perimeter Park South,
425-N
Birmingham, AL 35243
(205) 967–4905

Richmond Software
711 Morrefield Park Drive,
Suite L
Richmond, VA 23236
(804) 320–3313

RMS Systems
Two Scott Plaza
Philadelphia, PA 19113
(215) 521–2817
(Recommended: AS-400)

Rubicon Technology
465 Fairchild Drive, Suite 215
Mountain View, CA 94304
(415) 962–9533

SAS Industries, Inc.
SAS Campus Drive
Cary, NC 27513–2414
(919) 677–8000

Scicon, Inc.
5555 San Felipe, Suite 600
Houston, TX 77056
(800) 451–9664
(Recommended: DEC Mini's,
IBM MF)

Service Infosystems
3699 W. Henrietta Road
Rochester, NY 14623
(716) 334–9126

Software Solutions Unlimited
5600 Wyoming Blvd. Suite 10
Albuquerque, NM 87109
(505) 828–9000

Spacesaver Software
10992 San Diego Mission
Road
San Diego, CA 92108
(619) 280–0447

Specific Design
21062 Brookhurst Street,
Suite 103
Huntington Beach, CA 92646
(800) 262–8988

SpecTec General, Inc.
1920 Main Street, Suite 200
Irvine, CA 92714–7200
(714) 955–3350

Stagg Systems
400 North 5th Street,
Suite 1510
Phoenix, AZ 85004
(602) 256–7740

Sundance Software, Inc.
84 Business Park Drive
Armonk, NY 10504
(914) 273–6440

Synergen Associates
2121 N. California, Suite 800
Walnut Creek, CA
94596–7396
(510) 935–7670

Syska & Hennessy
115 Fifth Avenue
New York, NY 10003
(212) 979–3600

Taylor Industrial Services
10035 11th Street, No. 1002
Edmonton, Alta.
Canada T5K 2MS
(403) 482–7547

Team Tech Systems
127 Michael Drive
Red Bank, NJ 07701
(908) 530–1805
(Recommended: Small PC's)

Tenera Corporation
1995 University Ave.,
5th Floor
Berkeley, CA 94704
(415) 845–5200
(Recommended: IBM MF,
Custom)

The System Works
1640 Powers Ferry Road,
Bldg. 11
Marietta, GA 30067
(404) 952–8444
(Recommended: Large PC's,
UNIX, HP, DEC)

Timesaver Systems
P.O. Box 4688
Portland, OR 97208
(503) 253–0098

Titan Software
275 Center Road,
One Titan Plaza
Monroeville, PA 15146
(412) 372–7008
(Recommended: UNIX)

Trow Consulting Engineers
1595 Clark Blvd.
Bramptom, Ont.
Canada L6T 4V1
(416) 793–9800

Jack Tyler Engineering
6112 Patterson Ave.
Little Rock, AK 72209
(501) 562–2296

UE & C Catalytic
30 S. 17th Street
Philadelphia, PA 19102
(215) 422–4139

Western Business Solutions
13500 SW 72nd Avenue
Portland, OR 97223
(503) 639–5693

WinterCress Development
15 S. Grady Way, Suite 203
Renton, WA 98055
(206) 228–0635

Index